More Praise for
80+ GREAT IDEAS FOR
MAKING MONEY AT HOME

"My business is helping small businesses grow. First, however, people can help themselves by starting on the right track with good, basic information. 80+ GREAT IDEAS FOR MAKING MONEY AT HOME is loaded with ideas to provide that good beginning. Don't get started without it!"

—HOWARD L. FLOOD
President and CEO
First National Bank of Ohio

"This is a great book to stimulate thinking about business possibilities. It will help anyone interested in starting a full or part-time home-based business."

—BARBARA R. HONTHUMB LANGE
Executive Director
Women's Entrepreneurial Growth
Organization

"Without doubt, the best book I have read or heard about the subject. I dare anyone of any age to pick up this book, begin reading, and not be changed positively."

—RONALD E. WALLEN
Chairman
FARMAX Corporation

80+ GREAT IDEAS
FOR MAKING MONEY AT HOME

A Guide for the
First-Time Entrepreneur

Erica Barkemeyer

IVY BOOKS • NEW YORK

Ivy Books
Published by Ballantine Books
Copyright © 1992 by Erica Barkemeyer
Illustrations copyright © Polly Leonard Keener 1992. Used by permission.

The contents of this book reflect the author's views and do not necessarily represent the opinions of any other individual. The publisher and the author disclaim any personal loss or liability caused by application of information presented in this book. The author is not engaged in rendering legal or other professional services. As emphasized throughout the book, it is considered imperative for any self-employed individual to be counseled by a competent attorney, accountant, insurance professional, as well as a reputable banker before forming a business operation, however small.

Contract forms in Appendix C are from the book *J. K. Lasser's Legal Forms for Smaller Businesses*, 1988. Used by permission of the publisher, J. K. Lasser Tax Institute/A division of Simon & Schuster, Inc., New York, NY 10023.

Names of interviewed individuals who requested anonymity have been altered.

Library of Congress Catalog Card Number: 91-29062

ISBN 0-8041-1081-6

This edition published by arrangement with Walker and Company.

Manufactured in the United States of America

First Ballantine Books Edition: July 1993

To my late husband, and to my late father,
who enlightened me early in life about
entrepreneurship, inventiveness, and creativity
and to the countless enterprising Americans who,
regardless of age, admirably pioneer new,
fulfilling business ventures with dedication,
imagination, and perseverance.

Contents

Part IV
Home-based Businesses for People with a Business Background

Part V
*Minibusiness Ideas for People with Teaching, Writing, and
Travel Experience*

Acknowledgments

My sincere thanks to
Jack Colman, Peter D'Attoma, Cecil and Joanna
Dobbins, Billie Ferguson, Grant and Ralph Geiger,
Herbert O. Jacobson, Kay B. Johnston, Ginny
Knoll, Vera Lowe, Glenn and Grace Mayes, Donna
Murray, Karl P. Schmidt, John Simler, Sandi Smith,
Eugene W. Stanks, Julia Topa, Ronald E. Wallen,
Roger Williams, Tracy Woll, Cathy Wood, and
Laurie B. Zuckerman; and to the chairman of
SCORE (Service Corps of Retired Executives),
Chapter 81, and his volunteer corps of business ex-
perts who provide free counseling to small business
owners within a three-county area. I also extend my
gratitude to the numerous resourceful men and
women I had the pleasure of meeting at fairs, exhibitions, shopping malls, art shows, and home-based
offices, who shared their business experiences with
me yet preferred to remain anonymous.

My special thanks to
Carolyn Hann for her editorial expertise, and Polly
Leonard Keener for sharing her talent by contributing
promotional artwork.

Foreword

Home-based businesses have been an important part of the world's economy since the beginning of time. Many large, well-established companies started as home-based businesses.

I am pleased at the large number of people of all ages who want to start small businesses or home-based businesses today.

At the end of the twentieth century, men and women live far past the traditional retirement age. Many want a second career. They have the prerequisites for starting businesses—health, physical agility, and mental alertness.

These retired entrepreneurs are joined in their quest for business success by new college graduates who want to start home-based businesses. In larger and larger numbers, college graduates don't seek employment in corporate conglomerates or established small businesses. They want their financial achievements to reflect their personal efforts. Consequently, they look to home-based businesses for the start of their careers.

A third group of potential entrepreneurs already have established careers; however, they want a change in their lives. These people often have the financial resources and the skills to start a home-based business.

I met hundreds of people in each of these categories

when I was leading small-business development conferences designed to help would-be entrepreneurs get started. Some conference participants had specific business goals: "I want to be a caterer," "I want to manage my own nursing home," or "I want to open a bakery."

Others knew they wanted to be in business but didn't know what they wanted to do. As a conference leader, I'd ask, "What work experience have you had?" "What do you like to do?" "What are your hobbies?"

Many responded: "I don't know what I want to do. I don't want to do what I'm doing now. I know I want to be in business for myself."

Unsure of what to do next, these men and women continued to follow their dreams of having home-based businesses. In the introduction to this book, *Your Own Home-Based Business: Getting Started,* Erica Barkemeyer lists options for those who are unsure of which career path to take. For those who know exactly what they want to do, she describes the starting place for new careers.

I once helped a woman who knew what she wanted to do in her second career. Known locally for her delicious cajun-hot cookies, she opened a bakery. She now sells her products to several supermarket chains. When we last talked, she noted the fringe benefits for the home-based entrepreneur. "I'm doing what I want to do," she said. "I have a good product to sell and regular customers. I've hired twelve people and I pay their salaries. Of the twelve I've hired, six were collecting unemployment benefits before I hired them. And I make a little profit for myself."

That's a first-rate success story. She pleased customers, created twelve new jobs, and made a profit.

This story illustrates the power of the home-based business movement. Erica Barkemeyer provides the first steps for those who want to explore it for themselves.

I have advice for the reader: Don't read only those sections that apply to your interests. Spend time with every chapter of this book. Erica Barkemeyer has sprinkled sound advice and mature wisdom throughout. The treasures are here for you to discover and to apply to your own home-based business.

　　　　　　　—David Ritchey, Ph.D., School of
　　　　　　　　Communications, University of
　　　　　　　　Akron, and Business Ethics
　　　　　　　　Columnist, *Akron Beacon Journal*

Introduction

Your Own Home-based Business: Getting Started

- Manufacturer offers 500 white-collar workers early retirement to forestall layoffs
- Automaker's cutbacks to hit salaried jobs
- Hiring outlook deteriorates
- Buyout or layoff is choice at tiremaker
- Plant closings dragging down the working class
- Women sharing a downward spiral

Can any newspaper reader ignore or escape the daily bombardment of jarring banner headlines like the ones above? Of course not! In fact, you, or someone in your family, may already be caught in today's economic crosscurrents. Or perhaps you are worried that your job may be in jeopardy at some time in the future. Whatever your situation, you have probably thought to yourself, wouldn't it be great to secure a continuous income on your own, without relying on the vagaries of companies and other employers.

Throughout the country, millions of enormously capable men and women desire economic independence in their respective fields of expertise. And countless resourceful young and mature people actively prepare themselves for the day when they can embark on a new path in business.

If you are one of them, this book was written for you. Its purpose is to guide you to future commercial independence by demystifying the world of self-employment and home-based minibusinesses. With the assistance of simple guideposts, you are being encouraged to survey the abundance of stimulating, low-investment, and profitable service businesses.

Home-based businesses grew out of the hundred-year-old cottage industry. During the second half of this century this steadily multiplying business sector emerged as a creditable, money-producing industry. Consequently, in the 1980s we witnessed an upswing of home businesses so dramatic that an official count could not keep up with the actual happenings in the marketplace. According to estimates published by the U.S. Small Business Administration (SBA), during the second half of the eighties the number of home enterprises ranged from two to five million, and are expected to climb to ten to twelve million by the mid-nineties. The percentage of home-based businesses operated by women has not been determined but is thought to be high.

But why should millions of young, middle-aged, or older Americans choose to work at home? The SBA gives some of the advantages: low risk, low overhead, a gradual start-up, in addition to a more flexible lifestyle, and greater control over working hours.

The 1980s home business explosion leaves the impression that every marketable idea may already have been exploited and converted into an easy-to-run service business. Currently, the gamut runs from consulting, counseling, catering, teaching, and sitting to renting, planning, organizing, assisting, and writing about almost anything. What else is there left to offer the public? There always are untapped wellsprings. By combining your own specific skills with your past experiences, and examining the business ideas profiled in this book, you can come up with a viable idea for the business that is uniquely yours. Evaluate its practicality, its application in your community, and pioneer it.

Ronald E. Wallen, Ph.D., chairman of FARMAX Corporation and nationally known motivational speaker, articulates his viewpoint on books: "At some point, you will say to yourself: Wow! I never thought of doing that. I'll bet I'm capable of doing that. I could make some great money and have a lot of fun if I gave this a try." He then asks: "Can you teach, or sell, or promote, or write, or organize, or arrange, or research? If you can, many possibilities await you."

On the subject of how small business entrepreneurship will affect an individual's life, Dr. Wallen contends: "You want to stay young? It's no secret that the best way to enhance your energy level and maximize your flexibility is to move! Exercise your body, stretch your mind, act on new opportunities. It's up to you either to start slowly and stay small, or to move quickly and grow big."

Perhaps you are considering setting up a minibusiness with your spouse or friend. Dr. Wallen, who is also a nationally known business consultant, especially values relationship-building in the small business world: "People who share common visions and a sense of purpose are people who develop strong, often intimate personal ties. To be successful in any business enterprise, the participants must communicate about details and be honest about feelings. These are the elements necessary to forge friendship. Friendship is the basis of all good relationships." And friendship is the key factor to think about when starting a business on your own.

Where to Find Ideas and Assistance

This book's carefully selected minibusiness opportunities are profiled in Parts I through V. This format will allow you to choose the miniservice that matches your interests, background, skills, time, and financial resources. At the same time, you will read about the experiences of other men and women who have traveled the road before you. All miniservices are listed in the Index for your convenient use.

Appendix A directs you to governmental agencies, organizations, and trade associations, all of which render information, support, or resources to new entrepreneurs. Appendix B offers selected listings of useful reading material on general business topics, authored by top professionals. Invest in several of these often reasonably priced books and booklets, and keep them handy for daily reference. Featured in Appendix C are samples of frequently used contract forms. Have your legal counsel review these contract forms for appropriate application in your business.

A home-based service operation, like any other business, is subject to local, state, and federal laws and regulations. Therefore, the essential first steps for any business are to contact local authorities, such as the municipal government (licensing, zoning, liability regulations), and county and state government offices (tax and business-related state laws). Learn about the local requirements prior to establishing your new service business.

It is imperative for any self-employed individual, regardless of the size of his or her business, to obtain counsel from reputable local professionals: an attorney (well-versed in business/corporation law), a certified public accountant, an insurance professional, and a banker. How-to or self-help publications on the market—no matter how well-meaning—cannot replace the locally based professionals who can render individualized counseling on complex business matters. A wisely selected local professional team—with whom you feel comfortable—not only will steer you through today's labyrinth of business regulations to protect you against loss but also will enhance your chances for commercial success.

You also stand a better chance of doing well in business if you have certain characteristics in common with successful small business owners. You can take stock of your interests, skills, and experiences with the assistance of the two U.S. Small Business Administration (SBA) booklets, *Going into Business* (MP 12), and *The Business Plan for Home-Based Business* (MP-15). The checklists in these publications not only will tell you how you measure up, but also will help you avoid costly mistakes. Inexpensive, informative SBA literature is listed in Appendix B, where you will also find the order information. Or go to your public library and take out *The Small Business Test* by Colin Ingram (Ten Speed Press). Your score on this test will reveal the truth about yourself and your prospects as a small business owner.

Entrepreneurs Come in All Ages

At any age, facing a juncture in life can be distressful. Perhaps you have exhausted your search for a new satisfactory workplace, or you are exploring opportunities for a second income, or you have had to settle for early retirement. As a result, you have been trifling for some time with lofty ideas for a second career, or have worked at unrewarding or short-term jobs, but you also have been pondering a number of practical ideas for a small business.

You have heard or read in the media about the stimulating success stories of businesspeople. Most attention is given to exceptional people who become full-fledged millionaires, some even in their retirement years. But in addition, in newspapers around the country, we read about the less dramatic successes of people who just aspire to a good living for themselves. They embark on often new, imaginative ventures to respond to specific community needs. You will read about them in the following chapters. Some may even live in your own neighborhood.

The marketplace welcomes and rewards these enterprising individuals. Some recent successes include:

- the *former teacher* who organized a now flourishing tutoring agency
- the *seventy-plus couple* who operate a thriving citywide house-sitting service
- the laid-off *production worker* who formed a cleanup contract service
- the *bookkeeper* who teamed up with a family member to run a group touring service

- the *homemaker* who teaches party cuisine
- the young *mother of two* who is doing exceptionally well in direct sales
- the young *furniture finisher* who carved a niche for himself in the lucrative antique refinishing business
- the retired *purchasing agent* who turned to free-lance writing of creative nonfiction

The list goes on and on. And what entrepreneurial attitudes aid both the young and the mature to perform so admirably in their new endeavor? Self-discipline, a readiness to take risks with new ideas and concepts, enthusiasm for the task at hand, effective time management—all play important roles.

Interestingly, the majority of successful small business owners love what they are doing. Can one ask for anything more? If you have been a closet-entrepreneur until now—step out into the sunshine of the market-place and begin to spread your entrepreneurial wings. It's one of life's great experiences you don't want to miss.

Best of luck as you embark on an exciting and successful adventure.

- Enjoy working at your own pace
- Enjoy growing recognition in your community
- Enjoy reaping the rewards that come from providing quality service
- Finally—enjoy being your own boss!

Part I

||► ◄||

Ideas for Entrepreneurs with Little or No Previous Business Experience

1

||➡ ⬅|||

Enjoy Garage and Yard Sales?
Become a Consultant

How many garage sales did you count in your immediate neighborhood last weekend? Three? Four? Six million or more garage sales are held in the United States every year, according to estimates by scholars Stephen M. Soiffer and Gretchen Herrmann in an article written for *Urban Life*. This adds up to an estimated sales volume of about $1 billion. Yet a surprising number of homeowners, trying to dispose of possessions they no longer need—or wanting to raise funds for special causes—are ignorant of sales practices. Some even loathe this type of activity. Right there is your chance! Use your knowledge to cash in while doing work you enjoy.

Perhaps you have held yard or garage sales in your own driveway, or helped a relative or friend with a moving sale. And, of course, there are those classified ads for auction and garage sales that you scan eagerly.

When the weekend comes, you enjoy driving through residential areas following homemade cardboard signs attached to trees and utility poles and leading to clusters of cars already parked alongside the sidewalk. Usually the only parking spaces left are around the corner on the next block. Yet you love to mingle with the crowd, observe, question, rummage, or bargain at such sales. And, back in your car, you may exclaim: "Golly, I surely would run the show differently!"

If you fit the above description, you can learn to become an expert in the thriving field of yard, moving, and estate sales. And if you are blessed with a healthy dose of salesmanship, you stand an excellent chance of turning such consultant's work into an enjoyable, lucrative part-time weekend activity.

A consultant is expected to organize this type of sales event. He or she handles all the details, from arranging the goods to pricing, making promotional recommendations, and advising on sales policies. In return, the consultant is entitled to a percentage of the total sales, which typically ranges from 10 to 25 percent. Standard practice is to have the owner/seller sign a simple written contract detailing the consultant's functions and compensation.

If you need to update your knowledge, follow a step-by-step self-instruction plan. Begin by attending a variety of neighborhood sales. Scrutinize various types of ware, from collectibles to worthless junk. Observe the arrangement of goods, note the pricing, and pay attention to the sellers, buyers, attendance, sales hours, and promotional efforts. Keep a notebook handy so you can jot down your observations—both the positives and the negatives—and add your own ideas on how merchandise could be moved more effectively.

Then check your local adult education services for classes on appraising, antiques, and collectibles. Such classes, teachers, and fellow students are an excellent source of information on this subject.

It is important to pay close attention to your community's residential sales regulations. In many municipalities the number and length of residents' yard sales are regulated by ordinances (e.g., three sales a year, each not exceeding three days). Consequently, ignoring local ordinances can result in fines for zoning violations.

Because practice makes perfect, venture out and assist relatives and friends in setting up their sales. After a few successful experiences, you should be ready to launch your own consulting service.

To promote your service, have business cards and flyers printed at a quick print shop and distribute them at neighborhood gatherings. Also tack them to bulletin boards of food markets, community centers, and churches. Finally, for several weekends place an inexpensive classified ad in your local daily's auction/yard sales section. At the same time, inquire at the paper's advertising department about the availability of a garage sales kit, which a number of newspapers distribute to their advertisers.

Suggested Reading

Hitchcock, Peggy. *The Garage Sales Handbook.* Babylon, N.Y.: Pilot Books, 1986. (Order from Pilot Books, 103 Cooper Street, Babylon, NY 11702.)

Jenkins, Dorothy H. *A Fortune in the Junk Pile.* New York: Crown, 1963.

Kovel, Ralph, and Terry Kovel. *Kovel's Know Your Collectibles.* New York: Crown, 1986.

Stevenson, Chris H. *Garage Sale Mania: How to Hold a Profitable Garage, Yard or Tag Sale.* Crozet, Va.: Betterway, 1988.

2

Like Interiors Sparkling Clean? Cleanup Contracting Might Be for You

Wasn't it just last weekend that you drove through the countryside and discovered a new attractive condominium development still under construction? And, scarcely a mile closer to town, didn't a half-finished office structure catch your eye? Maybe you wondered who transforms the messy interiors of new buildings into acceptable "move-in" condition.

Although building subcontractors and tradespeople are obligated by contract to give their customers a finished building in clean condition, the fact is that they never do! A thorough cleanup is usually needed. What a great opportunity for an energetic, healthy person to set up a profitable, seasonal cleanup service.

Take the example of Leonard Hicks, a vigorous, no-nonsense individual who likes to do things with his hands. Several years ago, when he was laid off as a production worker, he set himself up in a seasonal cleanup contracting business in the Northeast. During the winter months he devotes his time to another minibusiness in Florida. His earnings are primarily based on a per-unit fee paid by the builder. Asked about the financial reward of cleanup contracting, he states that his income is "quite satisfactory."

6

It's a fact that new building and home cleanup jobs vary markedly in difficulty and scope. Therefore, labor charges—subject to regional fluctuations—must be carefully estimated; sometimes they are based on the number of hours worked plus the cost of supplies. Contact construction business officials in your area to find out local fees and cleanup standards.

Almost all services furnish cleaning supplies, tools, and other aids. As the need arises, movable appliances and aids, such as stepladders and scaffolding, are obtained from rental agencies. Adequate transportation, such as a pickup truck, is essential.

Because the demand for cleanup services increases during the peak of the season, you may have to look for outside part-time help. The ideal is a reliable service crew made up of your own family members. Any reinforcement with hired help from a temporary help agency requires not only strict supervision of workers but also exact calculation of labor costs. Before hiring outside help, try to figure out whether this will be cost efficient for you. You must be assured of a reasonable return on your own invested labor. Exception to the rule: occasionally a building contractor, pressed to meet contractual deadlines, is willing to increase the allocation for cleanup contracting.

All service owners agree that a cleanup service is hard and often tedious work. It includes scraping, washing, waxing, vacuum cleaning, and sometimes outdoor cleanup. Remember that assertiveness and supervision are vital if the cleanup crew is expanded. As in any trade or service, efficiency and reliability will assure you new business through referrals.

There Will Always Be a Market for Quality Cleaning

Render quality service and you will succeed even in a competitive service field. This is the motto of Roger Williams, owner of a commercial and residential cleaning service in a midwestern city. A thorough technical training qualified Roger for the trade, yet when starting his new venture, he lacked business know-how to carry on successfully. Now, looking back after operating the home-based service business for almost three years, the friendly thirty-year-old remembers receiving helpful business advice from SCORE counselors. At this point, improved managerial skills and time management, as well as temporary part-time workers, allow the service owner to accept a larger number of commercial clients. Roger is determined to expand his venture one new client at a time. He is confident that his quality service will ensure ample future business regardless of the competition.

Business cards, circulars, and a few classified ads should become part of your service promotion. Advertising will get your service business off to a good start. Also, bring your contracting business to the attention of area building contractors, real estate developers, and all businesses and services that cater to the building trade.

Cleanup services are not yet common in certain regions. With the assistance of local professionals, find out the license requirements in your area, as well as tax and other liability regulations.

Suggested Reading

Aslett, Don. *Cleaning Up for a Living.* White Hall, Va.: Betterway, 1988.

Consumer Guide, ed. *The Fastest, Cheapest, Best Way for Cleaning Everything.* New York: Simon & Schuster, 1980.

Griffin, William R., and John G. Davis. *How to Sell and Price Contract Cleaning.* 2d ed. Seattle: Cleaning Consultant Services, 1988.

3

Sharpening Tools: A Service with a Cutting Edge

Picture the following, if you will: a precious, long holiday weekend lies ahead of a fellow, let's call him Bob. Just perfect to finally finish that carpentry project he started more than a year ago. After a leisurely breakfast, Bob is ready to get started. Suddenly, much to his chagrin, his circular saw isn't working properly. A dull blade? No doubt. Unexpectedly, Bob's tightly scheduled weekend plans come to an abrupt stop. Annoyed, he walks outside and decides to finish mowing the lawn. During the first ten yards, however, Bob discovers strands of uncut grass. The blade of his rotary lawn mower is dull. Oh no, not again!

Does the above scenario sound familiar? If so, you'll probably want to skip this chapter. But if you are one of those handy homeowners who can sharpen almost anything, the idea of setting up a part-time tool-sharpening service may appeal to you and be worth exploring.

And the market potential for such service? There are countless household and workshop tools with cutting or working edges. Household tools include knives, scissors, spatulas, shovels, can openers—even screwdrivers, fishhooks, ice skates, ice picks. Many households own woodworking tools, such as handsaw, power saw, chisel, plane, shaping tools, scraper, drill bits, boring tool. Add to the above the large number of households that own a variety of garden tools, such as rotary lawn mower, hedge clipper and shears, hoe, rake, pruning saw, cultivator, garden tiller, and more. That totals at least ten items per small household and twice as many objects per larger suburban household. Moreover, countless tools are being used in small workshops and businesses right within your part of town. Since all such tools must be periodically maintained, repeat business is guaranteed. What a promising market!

Although you may have sharpened a variety of tools in your home workshop, it is vital to keep abreast of the latest sharpening techniques. Any public library branch carries a multitude of books on the subject. While reading about these techniques, practice them on your own tools or those of your friends.

If necessary, bring your home workshop up to good

working standards before making a small investment in sharpening tools. Basic sharpening tools include sharpening stones, various files, abrasives, a good bench grinder with attachments, as well as protective safety equipment.

Check local stores to find out the current rates charged for various sharpening jobs. And note that accurate labor estimates are essential if your new service business is to be profitable. Also check that your home-based service will conform with your area's zoning law, and investigate local licensing and tax regulations.

Start out slowly. At first, take on customers in your own neighborhood. As with any new home-based service, your promotion can start with inexpensive classified advertising in your local newspaper and neighborhood newsletters. Next, distribute flyers in residential areas. Then tack service announcements to bulletin boards of food markets, apartment buildings, and senior citizens' complexes. After introducing yourself to managers, leave flyers at hardware stores, garden centers, feed and supply stores. Develop your subcontracting business with retail stores on a one-at-a-time basis. A good place to start is your neighborhood hardware store and garden supply center. These promotional efforts should be sufficient to get your tool-sharpening service off the ground.

Suggested Reading

Davidson, Glenn D. *Tool Grinding and Sharpening Handbook.* New York: Sterling, 1985.

Geary, Don. *How to Sharpen Anything.* Blue Ridge
    Summit, Pa.: Tab Books, 1983.
Walton, Harry. *Home and Workshop Guide to Sharp-
    ening.* 2d ed. Popular Science Book. New York:
    Harper and Row, 1976.

4

||||➡ ⬅||||

Weave Durable Seating for
Profitable Chairs

Contrary to common belief, you don't have to look
very far to find beautiful period or heirloom chairs,
stools, or benches. They may grace a charming living
room, quaint bedroom, even a country kitchen in the
house next door, across the street, or around the corner.
But when chair seating needs to be rewoven, how long
does it take to find someone who can do a good job? It
depends, of course, on where you live. When I needed
the service, it took me two full days of research and numerous calls before I discovered a person capable of
doing quality recaning work. It's a rare trade indeed,
and by no means overcrowded!

Are you an individual who enjoys working creatively
with natural materials? Weaving attractive seating can
give you not only pleasure but also a sense of accom-
plishment. A great variety of materials, such as cane,

rushes, willow, seagrass, or even whipcord, are readily available through supply houses throughout the country.

The roots of this traditional craft date back to the sixteenth century; it gradually faded into oblivion. Then, earlier in the twentieth century, the craft was reintroduced into the seating trade. Decorative caning enhances furniture, and, surprisingly, its durability is now being rediscovered and appreciated in contemporary seating. With the demand slowly growing, the financial reward for producing creative and practical seating on a part-time basis is very satisfying.

According to people trained in the craft, chair caning is not difficult to learn. The main requirements are carefulness and patience. The weaving cannot be done hurriedly or carelessly. It is done in stages, each of which must be completed before proceeding to the next stage.

The investment in caning tools is minimal. Tools consist of penknife, small hammer, scissors or side cutters, small stiletto, clearing tool (similar to a screwdriver), pegs, round-nose and flat-nosed pliers.

If you have never attempted caning but want to learn the skill, here's what you should do. First, contact your public library for books on the subject. Caning and other types of seating are also extensively covered in craft and hobby paperbacks displayed on bookstore shelves. These richly illustrated books will encourage and inspire you. Also inquire at your local YMCA or adult education center—most likely an active caning work group or class meets there regularly. During the early stages of your studying, you should practice the craft on your own, or your friends', chair seating. With experience, you will find your weaving speed improving.

At that point, you will be able to charge locally acceptable per-unit fees, based on an hourly rate plus the cost of materials. Calculate your time carefully to ensure a reasonable profit. Make sure your fees are in line with the going rates for this service in your own and neighboring communities. Also check your area's zoning law and examine the local licensing and tax regulations.

Announce the opening of your service with a flyer distributed to businesses, such as carpenter shops, furniture refinishers, antique dealers, interior decorators, and furniture stores specializing in period furniture. These establishments either will refer customers directly to you or may consider subcontracting the recaning work needed by their clients.

Suggested Reading

Brown, Margery. *Cane and Rush Seating.* New York: Larousse, 1976.

Johnson, Kay. *Chair Seating: Techniques in Cane, Rush, Willow, and Cords.* London: Dryad, 1988.

Sober, Marion Burr. *Chair Seat Weaving for Antique Chairs.* Plymouth, Mich.: Balch, 1964.

5

IIII➤ ◄IIII

Watch Clients' Homes: A Security Opportunity

Even at the risk of upsetting a normal home or family life, some people prefer making a living during night hours, when they seem to function best. Others manage to work quite well either day or night. Do you belong to one of these two groups?

If you also happen to be laid off or retired from professional security or investigative services, are in good physical condition, and if you have flawless employment or personal references, an individualized security miniservice might appeal to you.

In spite of the abundance of high-technology home security systems on the market, many homes are not protected against break-ins, or vandalism, when owners are out of town. Without a doubt, homeowners are aware of the vulnerability of their property. For that reason, many are looking for alternative sources of protection. One option is an around-the-clock house sitter for absentee homeowners, an increasingly popular service profiled in Chapter 14. Another choice is to engage an hourly security service, some of which are *one-person security operations.*

Al Bowman, a mature but healthy outdoorsman with an aura of self-confidence and dependability, estab-

15

lished himself in the relatively new home-based security business after being laid off from the security force of a manufacturing plant. In excellent health and with unblemished references, Al had planned to join one of the professional security or detective agencies. However, he soon found out that these establishments favor younger recruits. For a couple of weeks, Al thought about his future plans. Curious to find out about opportunities for a home-based service, he contacted several security businesses in his hometown. What he learned was encouraging. He received plenty of expert advice and valuable suggestions. Shortly after, Al started a one-man operation which grew from a part-time activity into a profitable full-time service business. Repeat business and word-of-mouth recommendations have contributed to his success.

Security experts agree that during the property owner's absence, the client's home must be visited several times during day and night hours. Aside from securing the home by checking outside doors and windows, it is important to maintain the appearance of normal home activities. These include opening and closing of window coverings, operating the lighting system, and activating entertainment equipment. The security service may also need to check any alarm systems on the premises, take in the mail, and perhaps even leave children's toys scattered outside the home. If desired, a client may give the service authorization to arrange for lawn mowing or snow removal. During the slow season, services can be expanded to include the care of pets and plant watering at additional cost.

Sometimes, the property owner's watchdog can pose a problem. Find out as much as you can about any dogs on the premises before concluding your agreement with the owner. Some service owners claim to have turned down security jobs because clients' dogs were uncooperative.

Most states have licensing, bonding, and liability requirements for security businesses, which must be carefully investigated. A competent local professional team can help you comply with the existing security and liability laws.

Homeowners interested in individualized security service are likely to be found in residential and suburban areas. The service can be extended to small commercial enterprises as well. I recommend having an advertising agency design an attractive pamphlet detailing the advantages of such customized service. The agency will advise you on how you can best reach the targeted homeowners and businesses. Invest in a thoroughly professional promotional approach; it will pay off handsomely.

As an alternative to a one-person security service, become an independent *marketing representative* for one of the nationally known manufacturers of security systems. Success in this field will largely depend on the size and economic structure of your hometown or neighboring communities, and of course, on your sales ability. Financial investment may include a sample inventory of the systems you are selling.

Suggested Reading

Home Security. Illus. Sidney Cooper and Anne Beller. Mt. Vernon, N.Y.: Consumer Reports Books, 1988.

Kelley, Clarence M. *Security for You and Your Home.*
Blue Ridge Summit, Pa.: Tab Books, 1984.
Roper, C. A. *The Complete Security Handbook.* Blue
Ridge Summit, Pa.: Tab Books, 1981.

6

IIII➤ ◄IIII

Motoring Miniservices: Pickup, Transportation, Delivery

There are countless people out there who build their
livelihood around automobiles. If you would like to become one of them, consider the following questions: Do
you love to drive? Do you enjoy working closely with
people? Are you a capable, reliable driver with an excellent driving record? Do you own a well-maintained
spacious car?

If you answered yes to these questions, a motoring
miniservice may be right for you. Any of the three motoring services profiled below can be developed into a
money-producing part-time business. Select the service,
or services, that appeals to you the most and that best
fits the needs of your community.

Car Pickup and Delivery Service

Every weekday in communities all over the nation
hundreds of car owners have prearranged service ap-

pointments with car-care providers. But many car dealers, gas station mechanics, and other car-care services do not offer rental cars or loaners to patrons. Wouldn't it be nice if these patrons had the option of hiring someone to drive their cars to and from the repair facility? That's where your pickup service fits in!

If such a service seriously interests you, begin by making the rounds of dealer service departments, gasoline stations, body shops, and other automotive-repair centers in your community. Talk personally to every shop manager, and point out how their business will profit from your future service. At the same time, inquire whether the businesses will allow you to put your brochures and business cards in their establishments. Ask all pertinent questions that are on your mind, invite suggestions, and record them carefully.

To maximize your service, perform the scheduled driving in tandem with your spouse, another family member, or friend. Have that person follow you in your own car to the client's repair facility. That way, you can handle a second assignment or perform other motoring services. Although gasoline and wear and tear on the car are added costs, this procedure will also increase your business volume.

Finally, printed service announcements should be distributed to all repair establishments and the community center. Also have them posted in food markets and on church bulletin boards, or in house organs of large employers in your community (including hospitals, utility companies, manufacturers, newspaper publishers, and educational institutions).

Passenger Transportation

Another type of motoring service transports individuals on a regular basis. Although taxis provide quick onetime, one-way transportation, they are not readily available in some locations or are too expensive to be used routinely. Yet adults of all age groups with no access to automobiles or to public transportation must find a way to satisfy their personal transportation needs. Many have daily, weekly, or monthly appointments at doctors' offices, hospitals, dentists, therapists, educational institutions, and meetings. On numerous occasions, these people would gladly patronize a dependable, individualized, regular, and friendly transportation service, if available. In addition, a great number of elderly car owners who do not drive at night or in heavy traffic areas are looking for a reliable, competent driver who can take them places in their own car—to lectures, social events, concerts, theaters, or nearby metropolitan shopping areas.

To test the need for such a service, make the rounds at hospitals, physicians' and dentists' offices, senior citizens' buildings, retirement communities, apartment buildings, private schools, and educational institutions. Talk to the various office managers and determine whether any demand exists for a regular motoring service. Emphasize the benefits that they, as well as their patrons, will reap from your future service. Request that they lend their support by allowing you to place printed service announcements on their bulletin boards or office counters.

Your promotional campaign should also include a few

inexpensive classified ads in your local newspaper or weekly suburban paper.

In case you combine the services of car pickup and passenger transportation, careful daily scheduling is essential. Under all circumstances, avoid overlapping of bookings. Your reputation is at stake!

Courier/Delivery Service

Have you ever heard or read about a quick citywide courier or delivery service for business letters and small packages that need to be at their destination within the hour? Flexibility, punctuality, and expedient scheduling are prerequisites for such a service. Thus it should be run by someone with a professional approach who can offer proficiency, dependability, and who has a good rapport with commercial patrons. Combining this service with other types of motoring services is not recommended.

Citywide letter and small package delivery can be a lucrative activity. Once the service is established, income can be locked in by obtaining client contracts for periods of six months or one year.

Survey the need for this type of service in your community. First find out whether similar services are operating in your area. Then check out the numerous institutions, smaller businesses, and professional offices without access to transportation vehicles and driver personnel that are likely to subcontract citywide courier deliveries.

The health-care field, for one, provides a major group of potential clients: hospitals (purchasing and lab departments), clinics, medical laboratories, photo processing labs, health-care provider offices, health agencies. And don't rule out the variety of professional offices—such as large law and accounting firms, title and insurance companies—that all require quick city deliveries. Other excellent prospects are advertising and printing businesses with art and layout studios, typesetting services, and full-service printers. Don't overlook professional secretarial/typing services. Let's round off the prospective client list with architectural firms, industrial designers, model builders, building contractors, and many more companies with business that is subject to rigid daily deadlines. Once you go into business, you will want to establish personal contact with the organizations' managers who select the citywide courier or delivery service for their employer.

Note that individuals interested in setting up this service can contact their local SCORE office (Service Corps of Retired Executives) and take advantage of the organization's free counseling in business matters.

All motoring services are subject to some regulations. Therefore, at the earliest stage of your planning, clarify your community's licensing and liability requirements. Bonding is a necessity in many areas. And your insurance agent should advise you on possible insurance needs.

To utilize a professional, yet economic, accounting system, contact certified public accountants specializing in a small business clientele and obtain quotations for monthly customer billings, or use a system that can be easily implemented by you or a family member.

Before drafting rate schedules for all listed services, run a cost analysis with the assistance of recommended Small Business Administration literature (see Appendix B).

For passenger transportation and courier/delivery services, spend the larger part of your small investment on a professional promotion campaign. Contact a few reputable advertising companies, and request quotations for designing a sales letter, envelope, service circular, and business card. Also investigate the costs for mailing the printed material to prospective customers in your area. Then let the agency advise you on how to follow up the mailings.

© Polly Keener 1991

7

||||▶ ◀||||

Drive to the Airport in Your Client's Car (or Your Own)

Many air travelers seem to have a story of misfortune similar to this one: Steve had a late start and a few snags on his way to the airport to catch a plane. After facing a clogged airport parking lot entrance, he finally parked his car at the periphery of the lot—but no shuttle was in sight when he needed one. Consequently, he missed the flight to an important meeting.

Steve would have made his flight had he entrusted his car and his ground transportation to an airport chauffeuring service. The driving requirements for this type of service are relatively few: driver's license, excellent driving record, and a well-maintained, spacious car. Further essentials are references confirming trustworthiness and reliability.

Such a service will be particularly in demand in heavily populated areas—smaller cities, townships, and suburbs encircling larger airports that lack adequate, secure parking facilities. And because using other types of limousine services or airport parking lots does not suit every traveler's needs and preferences, there is a good opportunity for someone who loves to drive to start an individualized miniservice.

Airport limousine services usually do not cover the

total metropolitan area served by central airports. And if they do, they shuttle passengers to and from major urban hotels while frequently operating only during certain daytime hours on weekdays. Limousine service is rarely available for weekend travelers, and individualized transportation service to major railway stations is practically nonexistent.

Many travelers, business or otherwise, are hesitant to leave their own car at an airport parking lot, where it may be exposed to extreme weather conditions or subject to damage or vandalism. Families who own just a single car are not likely to want to keep it at the airport for any length of time. Furthermore, many air travelers dislike the hassle of getting their luggage to the terminal when they have to use a faraway parking space. When such travelers are unwilling or unable to have a friend or family member drive them to and from the airport, they must find other means of ground transportation.

Nowadays it's not unusual for small groups of three or four senior citizens to make a tour of other countries. They need transportation to the nearest airport for the flight to a national hub airport, where they will join an international touring group. Upon their return, they will need to be picked up at their local airport.

The airport-chauffeuring service requires you to drive the traveler in his/her car to the airport, dropping the individual off with luggage in front of the terminal's main entrance. Then you return the car to the traveler's home. (The same service can be offered to railway travelers.)

Advantages of such service are manifold, and the convenience of individualized chauffeuring service is obvious. Even more important, it gives the traveler peace of mind about punctual arrival at the airport and the care of his/her own car. Finally, the savings over costly airport parking fees are substantial.

Motoring service regulations vary from state to state. Your area's motor vehicle bureau can tell you whether such chauffeuring requires a special license and commercial insurance coverage. Most likely, bonding will be necessary because you are going to be entrusted with your client's car. Remember, though, that bonding is a good point to stress in your promotional material.

Before you establish your fee schedule, investigate the going rates in your area for airport limousine services and similar transportation establishments. Then analyze your expenses; you must net a reasonable profit and be compensated for working at odd hours.

To promote your new part-time venture, you may want to start with inexpensive classified ads in your local daily and weekly newspapers. Have a circular printed in a quick print shop. Leave flyers and business cards with travel agencies and the local automobile club. By all means, include hotels, motels, and inns to supplement their current limousine schedule, provided they offer this service. Particularly during your start-up period, zero in on weekend transportation needs. If necessary, utilize your own safe transportation vehicle. Gradually extend your promotion to include corporate travel departments, retirement communities, senior living centers, social and civic clubs. And finally, contact the airport management to promote your service at various locations in the airport.

8

||||▶ ◀||||

Demonstrate the Newest Product
on the Market

Have you always enjoyed selling, relishing the
throngs of people crowding your sales space? Remember sales presentations, particularly those to discerning
audiences? Or perhaps you gained sales experience year
after year at the annual fund-raiser of your club or
church, where you outperformed fellow volunteers. Regardless of your age, you can take advantage of the opportunities to turn your natural sales ability into a
lucrative part-time or full-time business.

The next time you are walking through a shopping
mall, large department store, or supermarket, take a
closer look at the men and women demonstrating a new
product. Not only do they demonstrate the product con-
vincingly, but they are likely to sell it as well. Such an
introduction process is generally limited to new merchandise of well-known and unknown manufacturers
who want to test a particular market area.

Product demonstrators have become a vast sales
force within our economic structure and are expected to
remain so for years to come. In order to demonstrate the
product effectively, the demonstrator must become thoroughly familiarized with the product and carefully follow the manufacturer's instructions. He or she must also

be able to supply and set up an inviting, attractive display, be it a table, booth, or stall, and provide tools and paper supplies. Visual aids, such as films, slides, posters, and printed literature, are generally furnished by manufacturers.

The product demonstrator operates very much on his/her own. You will find this person independently working at trade shows, exhibitions, product fairs, convention centers, in just about every shopping mall, as well as in department stores and supermarkets.

Before starting work as a demonstrator, the individual must sign a contract with the manufacturer. The first part of the agreement itemizes the location, duration, and display details of the demonstration. The second part records the time-based remuneration for demonstration and, in case of product selling, the sales commission presented as a percentage of net sales.

Notice that manufacturers offer two different presentations: one assignment type calls for demonstrating the product(s), another demonstrating and selling the product(s) at the same time. Therefore, it is important to examine carefully the payment rates for both types of services before signing any contract. If you are skilled in selling, the demonstration plus selling service is most likely the more lucrative activity.

The range of products is extensive—anything from cheeses, popular low-cholesterol spreads and sauces, to a variety of cosmetics, fashion accessories, to home tools, household and car gadgets, and home appliances. You may have to prepare and display cut-to-size merchandise samples and answer questions about product ingredients and recipes. If you demonstrate cosmetics, you may have to apply a dab of lotion, perfume, or makeup on the visitor's wrist. If you are working with household products, you may have to demonstrate the latest type of floor and carpet cleaner on a dirt-covered floor sample. Whatever the product, you must present it to the curious shopper in a professional and skillful manner.

One of the secrets of success is to approach those manufacturers that offer new products with mass appeal. Some of the hot-selling items include home and garden gadgets, as well as novelties that appeal to students, office workers, and computer fans. Products that cater to current fads, such as gourmet cooking, fitness, home security, pet grooming, and home entertainment are likely to become top sellers.

Your chances for success are further enhanced by astute observation, flexibility in presentation of sales pitch, a good-looking display, and a professional manner with the public. A demonstrator must attract the passing shopper's attention and persuade him/her to buy the product. Most demonstrators who sell products are determined to fulfill the manufacturer's sales quota, if there is one. This can net the demonstrator a respectable sum for a day's work.

If you are uncertain whether product demonstration is for you, take a few demonstration assignments as a recruit of a store marketing service, as described in the paragraphs at the end of this chapter. Or sign up with a temporary employment agency for several assignments in shopping malls or exhibitions. Then, if you still wish to become a product demonstrator independent of any marketing service, consult first-rate marketing magazines on library shelves, manufacturers' directories, or let a knowledgeable librarian steer you to promising manufacturers that you can contact. Also watch closely the "Wanted-Sales" ads in your local newspapers. Manufacturers frequently run classified ads to attract new demonstrators.

As an independently working demonstrator you should investigate at your county's tax office whether you need to take out a vendor's license to comply with state and local sales tax regulations. And if you will be applying cosmetic products in your demonstration work, find out whether your state requires that you take out a license to do so. Competent local professionals will aid you in setting up your independent demonstration service.

The nineties will see the broadening of a new trend, now very much evident in large metropolitan areas. Former experienced product demonstrators, frequently with the help of qualified family members, are establishing so-called *store marketing services*. Prerequisites for setting up such service are business knowledge and managerial and negotiating skills because the owners' primary goals are to expand their staff of recruited product demonstrators and to become a respected and decisive liaison between manufacturer and the retail trade (these services mainly deal with supermarkets and other grocery stores), as well as the consumer.

In some regions the marketing services have already grown intensely competitive. Such a business requires capital of at least ten thousand dollars and, importantly, liability insurance coverage in excess of one million dollars. A small store marketing service maintains a minimum of four accounts; these are manufacturers whose products are demonstrated in stores by service personnel. The manufacturers compensate the service with a flat fee per store demonstration, a figure which is seldom divulged to the public. Payment by corporations for services rendered can be expected within sixty days from billing date.

The average marketing service maintains a demonstration staff of at least one hundred self-employed men and women. They are called to do in-store product demonstrations occasionally on Thursdays, but mostly during Friday and Saturday store hours. These independent demonstrators meet their own display needs (table, paper supplies, disposable utensils), while the store provides the merchandise. The pay for either product demonstrating or selling is a flat fee per day. The amount varies from one region to another. In the Midwest the compensation averages $50 per day.

It requires a computerized system for the marketing service owner to keep track of the accounts, and of the legion of recruited demonstrators: their availability, demonstration scheduling in various stores, last-minute substitution, and accounts payable. The service owner also passes on to the staff demonstration instructions and sometimes provides light training to the part-time crew. It is also important for the service owner to cultivate good relations with store owners or managers.

Only at start-up time is it necessary to recruit the self-employed product demonstrators through local newspaper advertising. Once a stable pool of qualified individuals has been established, new applicants are attracted by word of mouth. The hiring is finalized with the signing of the independent contractor agreement between service owner and product demonstrator. Organizing a store marketing service can be a lucrative and challenging task for the right person with financial resources.

Suggested Reading

Girard, Joe. *How to Sell Anything to Anybody.* New York: Warner Books, 1979.

Johnson, Spencer, M.D., and Larry Wilson. *The One Minute Sales Person.* New York: Avon Books, 1984.

9

Shop for and Deliver Groceries to Satisfied Customers

A service to shop for other people? Indeed. Do you enjoy walking through supermarkets and grocery stores, keenly observing display shelves, noting tables packed and aisles clogged with familiar and new brand name products? Are you proud of your ability to spot brisk fluctuations in price and, of course, to ferret out genuine bargains? And, equally important, do you take pleasure in working with people and have access to a well-maintained stationwagon or hatchback? If so, you have all the makings of a success in the shopping-for-people service field.

During the past few years the demand for shopping assistance has multiplied. Increasingly, two-career households and homes headed by a single working parent are looking for assistance in a variety of time-consuming household chores. Add to these prospects the temporarily housebound, permanent shut-ins, and the handicapped who cannot do their own grocery shopping or perform other necessary errands. Cashing in on this growing demand, enterprising people are now setting up a variety of shopping services that require little financial investment. This profile focuses on grocery shopping and nearby pickups for clients on a regular basis. For errand and runabout service, see Chapter 10.

The service owner typically asks the client for a list of items to be purchased, and about store preference. He or she then proceeds with the shopping and afterward drops off the merchandise at the client's kitchen. The trip to the food market may include stops to run other errands. The client may request pickups at a discount store or pharmacy, or take-out food from a restaurant or fast-food establishment.

Some service owners charge a flat fee for their services—for example, 10 to 12 percent of the grocery total with a reasonable minimum charge of, let's say, $6.00. Pickups at stores other than groceries are $3.50 per stop, or three stops for $5.00. Naturally, charges vary from one community to the next. They depend to a great extent on the size of the area serviced: rates are generally higher in large cities. An established shopping service should be able to handle several shopping jobs simultaneously, boosting income accordingly.

The development of a stable and loyal clientele is essential if your shopping service is to be profitable. To attract clients, start with the printing of a colored flyer that describes the service, lists the fee schedule, and

mentions that references are available upon request
(prospective clients want the assurance that you are
trustworthy). Since the infirm and the elderly tend to
need your service more than the general population,
consider giving a fee discount to those on a fixed
income—a popular promotional measure.

Communities Need Shopping Services

For several years, shopping services have been germinating in California and numerous other states. Jack Colman, a people-oriented individual laid off from his job at a department store, had heard about shopping services through relatives. Determined to open a community-oriented home-based miniservice after his layoff, Jack formed less than a year ago his Personalized Shopping Service, which attracts more and more of the elderly, the handicapped, and the temporarily homebound. Perceptive and flexible, the new service owner recognized the demand for transportation of clients to health-care appointments, shopping malls, and entertainment sites, in addition to personalized grocery shopping. While others fail, Jack introduces new problem-solving shopping and transportation ideas—and successfully presses forward.

Contact managers of grocery stores and food markets in your area. When speaking to them, emphasize the benefits they'll reap when you shop at their stores on your clients' behalf. Then ask for their permission to display your promotional material at their facilities. Your flyers should also be distributed door-to-door in neighborhoods that show interest in your service. In addition, flyers can be posted on bulletin boards at apartment houses, senior citizens' buildings, and retirement communities, and distributed to social, corporate, church, and professional organizations, as well as health-care offices.

To announce your new service, you may want to run a few classified ads in daily and weekly newspapers. Other suitable publications for classified advertisement are newsletters that target shoppers, home buyers, and senior citizens.

Finally, contact shopping service owners in neighboring communities—most will be willing to share valuable experiences. But do your own research on local license and tax regulations.

10

||||➡ ⬅||||

Doing Errands for Profit

Practically nonexistent a decade ago, *errand and runabout service,* though still in its infancy in some areas, can now become a solid supplemental income base for enterprising individuals everywhere.

Luckily, you don't have to look very far for customers. The numbers of prospects are growing—on the one hand, homebound people (the handicapped, the elderly, those who are temporarily incapacitated); on the other, busy career singles and couples. If given a choice, the majority of homebound persons prefer a dependable, individualized order-in service by a friendly and accommodating individual over any impersonal taxicab service, where the taxi driver must incorporate order pickup and delivery with many other driving tasks.

In many parts of the country resourceful men and women offer a miscellaneous errand service on a subscription basis. For a weekly or monthly flat fee, this service can include order pickup at drugstores, trips to the bank, post office, library, and specialty stores. It may also include paying bills or making stops at municipal or county offices. For example, a weekly or semiweekly errand service for the homebound can center on the grocery shopping at neighborhood food markets, with occasional pickup of prescription drugs and takeout food.

Any service of this type has the potential to grow gradually by adjusting itself to local community needs. Take a survey within your community before advancing the service in any direction. If there is an apparent growing demand for some specified in-home tasks, expand the service accordingly. You might even consider becoming the coordinator of a more comprehensive *service network* and hiring senior citizens part-time for individualized in-house or outside chores. It makes good business sense to observe the activities of similar services in your area; inquire and learn from their experience.

The start-up investment is low—a dependable, spacious car, and a reliable scheduling and billing system. At the promotional end of the business, have attractive business cards and a circular printed. The latter should detail your various services and charges. Include community references in your promotional material; your future clients will appreciate it. Direct the distribution of your service announcement toward apartment houses, senior citizens' buildings, and retirement communities. Likewise, approach social service agencies, hospitals, health-care offices, churches, synagogues, and community centers.

Once you are ready to include busy career persons, reach out to them through luxury apartment complexes, condominium developments, health and fitness clubs, country clubs. Also try to get your service announcement tacked to bulletin boards of professional offices—brokerages, law and accounting firms, real estate agencies, and local corporate offices. If the latter publish house organs, see if you can persuade the editors to publish a story about your service.

Lastly, examine existing local licensing and tax laws and, depending on the extent of your errand service, look into the need for bonding and insurance coverage with the help of local professionals.

11

||||➤ ◀||||

Put Your Green Thumb Talents to Work

Yes, there is a perfect money-making service for men and women who dote on flowers and houseplants! You know the kind of people. Their lush green plants always seem to be in bloom or to grow profusely. They invariably grow showroom-quality foliage. And nowhere in their home is the slightest evidence of droopy fronds, wilting ivies, or limp Dieffenbachias!

The greening of the American home began in the seventies and is still flourishing. From blossomy hanging plants in picture windows, lofts, and luxuriant winter gardens to jungle-inspired greenery in bathrooms and grovelike atrium settings, all need careful and regular attention.

Frequently, the homeowner's financial investment in indoor greenery has been substantial. And today's admired vegetation is often the result of years of tender loving care. But who takes over when the owner goes on vacation? Or on longer business trips? That's why "care-for plant" in-home services have mushroomed in recent years.

You don't have to be a degreed botanist to set up such service. You should, however, have an all-around knowledge of indoor plant life. If necessary, broaden your knowledge by studying the latest publications on houseplants; there is no shortage of excellent sources in your public library. Then visit some larger florists, plant specialty shops, and nurseries, familiarizing yourself with the various houseplants that are currently popular and with their proper care.

Caring for indoor plants is not difficult. Aside from watering and feeding, the care involves occasional polishing of the foliage and checking the light exposure. Depending on season and region, the assignment may include checking room temperature or watering outdoor plants, as well as operating lawn sprinklers.

The plant-care service is a flexible one. Once established, it can be readily expanded and, among other things, become a supply source for plant lovers' accessories. Wholesale supply houses and craft dealers are often willing to let the service owner have some profitable accessory items on consignment.

Investigate similar services in neighboring communities and establish your fee schedule in accordance with charges accepted in your area. Established local professionals should aid you in organizing your new service business.

Take your newly printed business cards and attractive flyers to garden supply centers, nurseries, plant specialty shops, and florist departments in supermarkets. Don't hesitate to enlist their support for your service, but make sure that they are not in competition with your service business. Clients can also be secured through community organizations, such as garden clubs, as well as upscale apartment buildings and condominium developments. And what about business offices? Many office personnel prefer not to be burdened with plant care; therefore, office managers will welcome a regular, knowledgeable caretaker.

Suggested Reading

Gardener's Answer Book. Sunset Books, Menlo Park, Calif.: Lane, 1983.

Houseplants. Sunset Books. Menlo Park, Calif.: Lane, 1983.

12

||||➡ ⬅||||

Love Dogs and Other Pets? Enjoy Them and Get Paid for it!

It's a fact. Pet owners, like other people, want to go on vacations and weekend trips. They also must deal with out-of-town business assignments. But what are they to do with their house pets? Deposit them at a kennel? In their search for alternatives, pet owners have recognized that animals often seem happier when left in their accustomed surroundings. But it's not always a viable option to have relatives, friends, or neighbors drop by the house every day and care for the pet.

Find a need and fill it! Aside from dogs and cats, there are innumerable small animals in need of home care. Some families own birds, fish, hamsters, and guinea pigs. Add to this list those families who keep larger animals, such as ponies or horses, in barns and shelters.

In-house service for pet owners encompasses basic animal care. Such care may require more than one visit per day. Yet the feeding, walking, or exercising of the pet(s), plus cleaning the animal's quarters, is not time-consuming.

Individuals in this line of work advise paying a visit to the prospective client's home before entering into any

The Pet Care People
Call 000-0000

We walk, sit, care
for your pet...

Best of
References

service agreement. Familiarize yourself with the animal(s) and surroundings. Accept the job only if the pet is cooperative and no other problems are apparent. Furthermore, discuss the subject of liability with the new client. You should also have the telephone number of neighborhood veterinarians on hand. Obtain the client's authorization to take the pet to its regular veterinarian in case an emergency arises.

Even if you start a small-scale service, have a simple duplicate form printed on which you can fill in the details of your agreement with the client—the duration of your services, service fee, possible purchases of supplies, and emergency care provision. After both parties have signed the document, hand the client the original and keep the copy for your files.

The generally accepted compensation for pet service is a flat per-day fee. For long-term care/walking services, fees are frequently based on a weekly rate. You may even grant discount rates to people on a fixed income or lower your rates during seasonal lows. These are both worthwhile advertising techniques. To make the service more profitable, take on additional long-term dog-walking business; busy career persons and the homebound are good prospects.

When writing your promotional circular, elaborate on all aspects of your service. If possible, add some references. The client wants to know exactly what care he or she can expect for the pet. Every pet owner wishes to contract the most reliable, individualized service.

It's important, for example, that you arrange for a capable, dependable substitute who can fill in at a moment's notice in case you become indisposed. Investigate your local license, bonding, and tax regulations with the assistance of local professionals. A reputable insurance agent can counsel you on adequate insurance coverage.

Business for this service can be generated through pet stores, pet-supply and feed centers, pet-training clubs, animal hospitals, pet-grooming stores, and veterinarians. However, take note of the fact that some establishments will compete with your in-house service.

Initially, place some inexpensive classified ads in daily newspapers and weekly neighborhood newsletters. Then distribute your business cards and flyers to apartment buildings, the local humane society, as well as retirement communities, social service organizations, residential neighborhoods, and suburban developments.

Interested in a different kind of pet care? Read about a new service idea in Chapter 33, "Animal Lovers: Here Comes the Pet Express."

Suggested Reading

Moran, Patti J. *Pet Sitting for Profit*. Pinnacle, N.C.: New Beginnings, 1987.

Nichol, John. *Complete Guide to Pet Care*. London: Christopher Helm, 1988.

Pet Care as Business

Doesn't "Puppy Love Pet Care" immediately impress you as a very caring place? This two-year-old, home-based professional pet-care and -taxi service is owned by the amiable and knowledgeable Cathy Wood, a former homemaker with a background in animal care. From the start, the service generated a business volume far beyond a one-person operation, and today trained family members assist the service owner in her lively daily activities. Among Cathy's clients are households with several pets or handicapped pets that require individualized, loving care. Equally brisk is Cathy's pet-taxi service to veterinarians, kennels, and even airports. The secret of this booming pet-care business? The owner urges those starting out in this expanding service field to keep studying animal care and behavior, communicating well with the client and always becoming acquainted with the pet(s) before the assignment.

13

||||➡ ⬅||||

Baby-sitters Register Here

"Quick! Quick! Where can we find a dependable baby-sitter for tonight?" Does it sound familiar? You have heard it many times. But have you always been able to do something about it?

Attractive money-making opportunities grow out of present-day needs. Here is an excellent chance for a special type of individual to profit from a part-time service useful to any community. The person starting a baby-sitting referral service, or registry, must enjoy the reputation of a responsible citizen within the community. Good organizational skills are the backbone of an efficient and profitable service.

Start out with inquiries at local county and community agencies about current license or certification requirements, as well as liability and other legal obligations. If you are seriously considering this activity, have competent professionals (attorney, certified public accountant, insurance professional) assist you in complying with local laws.

One way of giving your service an easily recognizable identity is to recruit exclusively mature and senior persons for the sitter service. At start-up time, a minimum of ten free-lancing sitters should be available. This number can be gradually increased as business grows.

Remember, the success and reputation of such a service depends to a large measure on the caliber of the sitters. To locate qualified persons, you may have to spread the word through local daily newspapers, churches, senior citizens' centers, seniors' organizations, and retirement and fitness clubs. Prospective sitters should have some background in child care. If applicants have not already taken a baby-sitting course at adult education centers or community colleges, encourage them to do so. Additional sitter requirements are health clearance from their physician and a minimum of three references, which must be carefully checked out. Sitter duties and accountabilities, as well as the client's responsibilities, should be examined in the literature listed at the end of this chapter.

Because service rates vary markedly from one area to another, make some inquiries in neighboring cities and check with local sitters about going rates in your area. In most cities the rate exceeds the hourly sitter's pay of $2. Besides, a number of additional sitting services justify extra charges. These include after-midnight-sitting service, holiday service, giving children meals, washing dishes, and other chores.

The owner of the baby-sitter service is entitled to a percentage of the fee he or she establishes and negotiates with the client family. The service owner has the choice of billing the client for rendered sitting services and then reimbursing the free-lancing sitter, or having the client pay the fee directly to the sitter, who in turn must pass on the commission share to the owner. Either way, there is a need for precise monitoring of the sitter, who may attempt to make direct deals with the client or vice versa. Exact recordkeeping and hiring trustworthy sitters help ensure success.

To attract clients to your referral service, distribute your printed detailed circular at homes in residential areas, civic clubs, churches, synagogues, local PTAs, pediatricians' offices, hotels, motels, and large employers. Also make use of the bulletin boards in apartment complexes and food markets. And at start-up time, run some inexpensive classified ads in local daily newspapers, weekly neighborhood papers, and shoppers' bulletins.

Suggested Reading

Benton, Barbara. *The Baby Sitter's Handbook*. New York: Morrow, 1981.

Eichenberger, Shirley. *Mother's Day Out: How to Start a Business That Gives Mothers the Day Off*. Overland Park, Kans.: Oak Hill, 1983.

Lansky, Vicki. *Dear Baby Sitter Handbook*. Deephaven, Minn.: Book Peddlers, 1990.

14

IIII➤ ◀IIII

If You Admire Lovely Homes, Start a House-sitting Service

Remember that graceful, Georgian-style home flanked by many-colored flower beds? Or that cluster of stunning contemporary condominiums with sun terraces built into the protective south slope of the Oak Hills terrain? How about living in any of these impressive homes for one or two weeks, or even longer? Impossible, you think?

Not at all! Wanted: energetic, trustworthy, and alert homemaker of good standing in the community. Do you fit this description? And can you leave your own living quarters on short notice? If so, the rapidly growing field of house-sitting may be for you. You will find it not only enjoyable but also financially rewarding.

When you set up an in-house service business, you offer a useful community service. Nowadays, when making vacation plans, a growing number of homeowners, some with children, others with house pets, are turning to these new house-sitter services. By no means is this limited to the summer months.

Today, one- and two-career families, couples, and single homeowners leave town year-round. They spend time in their vacation home or their own resort condominium. They go on cruises or on a boating vacation.

Leave Them In Our Care

HOUSES · CHILDREN · PETS
  · Efficient
  · Experienced
  · Affordable
      800-1110
BONDED ~ REFERENCES
An All-Senior Sitting Service

Some take trips to play winter sports or embark on holiday tours; others go on safaris.

The house sitter moves into the house or condominium the moment the owner is ready to leave it and lives there until his or her return. The sitter's duties vary with each assignment. In some instances, the job may mean taking care of children. However, more often it means just caring for a pet (or pets), watering the plants, taking care of telephone calls and mail, and giving the home a lived-in appearance. Depending on region and season, duties may also include supervising backyard care by an outside contractor.

As a conscientious homemaker you will, of course, apply the same care to a client's home as you would devote to your own. And while you are compensated handsomely, you will have plenty of time to pursue your own interests.

If this activity appeals to you, first find out whether such services are already being offered in your community. If so, contact the service owners and inquire about locally established sitting rates. The fee is commonly based on a per-day rate plus special charges for added individualized service.

One of the advantages this business offers is that it can be started as a one-person part-time activity. Once it is established and you gain some experience, you may very well consider providing a full-time service to meet the growing demand. At that point, you can expand the business by recruiting qualified house sitters. Again, you don't have to look far. Among the increasing number of mature persons, you will find many suitable recruits who will welcome a pleasant opportunity to augment their income. Then, go one step further: while *managing a number of sitters* and receiving a percentage of their fees, simultaneously house-sit at a client's home of your choice.

If you are serious about such a home-based business for yourself, or contemplate starting one together with your spouse or a friend, I recommend that you order and study the beneficial manual listed at the end of this chapter. It's the only book of its kind and can be purchased only through direct-mail ordering. The author of the manual, a teacher and former peace corps member turned entrepreneur, has successfully operated a home-sitting service since the early eighties. Her informative publication tells you how to start your own business and how to keep it running smoothly and profitably. Sample forms, contracts, checklists, and applications are included as well.

Prospective clients can be attracted through inexpensive classified ads in local daily and weekly suburban papers, as well as shoppers' newsletters. As soon as your printed flyers—be sure to include the line "references upon request"—are available, distribute them in residential and suburban areas. Pass them out at condominium developments, country clubs, health spas, women's clubs, civic organizations, churches, and synagogues. Don't neglect to introduce yourself to travel agents, real estate brokers, and Welcome Wagon organizations.

Suggested Reading

Poston, Jane N. *How to Run a Housesitting Business.* Tucson: Housesitting Security Service, 1986. (Order from Housesitting Security Service, 1708 E. 9th Street, Tucson, AZ 85719.)

Part II

Home-based Businesses and Services for Anyone with Technical Skills

15

IIII➤ ◀IIII

Choices for Those Skilled in Woodworking

Remember the last showcase-home tour in your city? How could a visitor ever forget the nineteenth-century mansion's center hall with its beautifully furbished woodwork and the polished wooden balustrade of the elegantly curved grand staircase? Also impressed upon the visitor's memory are the restored exquisite antique furniture pieces tastefully arranged on stately Persian rugs. Moreover, quite unexpectedly, at the refurbished third floor, the clever zigzag-pattern paneling of a young man's studio grabs the attention of visitors.

The decorative details were noted and appreciated by everyone on the tour, but especially admired by those with occupational ties to, or hobby interests in, woodwork refinishing, furniture restoration, or carpentry. If you are a craftsperson by trade or a skilled hobbyist, channeling your skills into a profitable part- or full-time service will bring personal satisfaction.

Begin with an analysis of your talent and work experience. What type of woodworking do you enjoy most? Be honest with yourself. If your present work methods seem inefficient, upgrade your knowledge—find out about the latest techniques, tools, and finishing products. You will be surprised at the wide selection of books on the subject in your public library.

Then practice diligently on some of your own or your friends' woodwork or furniture pieces. Once you have gained confidence in your work, you will quickly become aware of your woodwork preferences. Not until then do you want to choose a specialized area for commercial pursuit.

If you are the imaginative type and like to create new and original pieces, or do *carpentry work* easily from designer plans or customer sketches, your success for a profitable minibusiness is practically assured. Scores of people are looking for someone to build customized computer furniture, home office built-ins, decorative book shelving, collection display cases, entertainment storage built-ins, Parsons tables, original coffee tables, window lambrequins, indoor plant display cases, or decorative wall paneling.

You can even go into mass production—if a hand-built item of yours has proven to be exceptionally successful. You have the option of subcontracting the production to a larger workshop, so that you can concentrate on distributing and selling the items at a gratifying profit. You may even consider the ultimate step: a truly novel and imaginative product can be protected by a design patent.

Two other fields with perpetual demand for qualified, self-employed craftspeople are *furniture refinishing* and *repair*, and the *restoration* of valuable woodwork in older homes and mansions. If you are one of those talented craftspersons who have proven themselves in restoring valuable antique furniture, by all means, go into this specialized, lucrative business.

It requires expertise, dexterity, and experience. You will be working not only with a fastidious private clientele but also with discriminating antique dealers. Thus you will be obligated to present references and photographs of previously restored pieces. Such specialized business is generally limited to metropolitan areas.

Before establishing service fees in any of these specialized fields, investigate work rates in your area. Certain jobs may justify hourly rates, while in other instances piecework charges are preferable. With extensive renovation jobs, it's not uncommon for the customer to act as the general contractor and to hire a self-employed carpenter as subcontractor. The remuneration may then be based on an hourly wage, plus materials, if furnished. Note that anyone affiliated with woodworking trades must furnish his or her own work tools when performing subcontractor work.

Piecework estimates require careful calculations because you want to make a reasonable profit. The job estimate must be submitted to the customer in written form, and upon its acceptance, both parties sign a binding work contract. In most communities contract forms can be obtained at printers of legal blanks.

Start your initial promotional efforts for all woodworking services by placing several classified ads in local and suburban newspapers. Second, have your neighborhood quick print shop assist you in designing a colored flyer that details your specific service and fees.

Many home renovation and decorating plans call for customized carpentry work. If this is your chosen field, introduce yourself to interior designers and at all stores with interior decorating departments. Also visit lumber and home centers, which can pass business your way when their customers ask them to recommend a carpentry service.

If you're setting up a furniture restoration and repair service, contact better furniture stores and interior design studios. They can generate considerable business for you. And don't overlook auctioneers. Their recommendations can result in valuable repeat business. Furthermore, historical societies, curators and custodians of museums and historic buildings should be made aware of your service as furniture and woodwork refinisher.

Once you have established a private and commercial clientele and demonstrated your craftsmanship and reliability, referrals will naturally lead to the steady growth of your minibusiness.

Lastly, the availability of an adequate workplace—your own or a rental property—is essential. And always comply with local licensing and zoning ordinances and tax regulations in your community. At the early stage of your business planning, consult a reputable accountant for help with recordkeeping, and let an insurance professional advise you on bonding and liability requirements.

Suggested Reading

Berqquist, Craig. *Carpentry Techniques, Finish.* San Francisco: Ortho Books, 1983.

Ratcliff, Rosemary. *Refurbishing Antiques.* Chicago: Regnery, 1971.

Williams, Jeff T., ed. *Carpentry Techniques, Basic.* San Francisco: Ortho Books, 1981.

16

Repair Small Appliances: Tinkering That Has a Payoff

Have you ever counted the scores of small electrical appliances and gadgets the average American household can't get along without? It seems no one ever bothered to take stock. Except for the utility companies, which, with the help of clever TV commercials, remind us of the arsenal of electrical contrivances we depend on in our daily routine.

It's debatable how indispensable electrical carving knives or can openers really are. However, a battalion of other devices, such as clocks, radios, coffee makers, blenders, toaster ovens, shavers, hair dryers, steam irons, electric blankets, determine the pace and contribute to the smooth functioning of our tightly programmed everyday life.

Do you have a knack for quickly putting your finger exactly on the problem of a nonfunctioning electrical item? And can you also fix it in no time? Perhaps you have an occupational background in electrical repair work? If so, you can easily, and with little investment, apply your skills to a part-time appliance repair service. It should provide you with a nice, steadily increasing income.

Work should be plentiful. Many consumers are disen-

chanted with exorbitant service charges at stores, let alone with the long waiting period for repair of indispensable household devices. Let's forget about the warranty; it usually has run out the day before the breakdown.

Pay a visit to your nearest public library and have a librarian assist you in finding up-to-date books or manuals on appliance repair. Also, bookstores carry the how-to variety of paperbacks on this subject.

The investment in tools should be minimal, particularly if you have done repair work in the past. In the beginning, if necessary, you may be able to rent tools or equipment. Use service centers, surplus stores, or appliance stores as sources to find tools and needed repair parts.

Part of your early business planning should be to study your community's zoning laws, as well as possible licensing and tax regulation for small services. In addition, contact an accountant specializing in small-business clients and have him/her set up an appropriate accounting system.

Your business emphasis should be on reliable, speedy service. Likewise, it is essential that you carefully estimate every repair job. You must be assured of a fair profit for your work. When you are ready to bid on repair-contract work for retail businesses, keep in mind that the pricing should be appealing. But don't compromise on an adequate labor-plus-parts profit margin.

Start your service promotion by placing some inexpensive classified ads in local daily newspapers and weekly community papers. The next step will be to tack single-page flyers on the bulletin boards of major stores, food markets, and apartment buildings. Then contact those small-appliance retailers and make your services known, provided no conflict of service interest is apparent.

Soon referrals will contribute to a steady flow of repair orders. The increased volume may even create a need for you to subcontract some of your private customer jobs. At this phase, if you so desire, you can make the transition to a full-time small appliance repair service.

Suggested Reading

Powell, Evan. *Complete Guide to Home Appliance Repair.* Popular Science Book. New York: Harper and Row, 1984.

17

Large Appliances Need Installers

Have you ever installed large appliances and enjoyed the challenge? Are you physically up to the task? What about your all-around installation know-how and credentials?

If you are an able-bodied person with extensive handyman experience, you may want to consider setting up an installation service. Since no two installation jobs are exactly alike and since it is necessary to deal with a diverse clientele, versatility and flexibility are prerequisites for success. On the plus side of the trade, there is plenty of installation work around. In most communities the prospects for a financially rewarding part-time or even full-time installation service are very good. Other aspects of this trade, repair and customizing of appliances, are getting increasing attention.

The demand for installation of large appliances plus smaller fixtures is steady through most of the year. Boosted by special sales before and after seasonal holidays, purchases of kitchen and laundry appliances occur year-round. Air conditioners and ceiling fans are purchased especially in the spring and early summer seasons.

And there is nothing wrong with going after a share

of the seasonal homebuilders' installation business. If you desire, you can approach both the consumer and the construction business, provided you can produce the credentials required by the construction trade and their fixture suppliers.

Assuming your installation knowledge and experience include basics in electricity, plumbing, and carpentry, you should acquaint yourself with up-to-date methods and products. Many adult education facilities feature refresher courses or advanced classes on the trade. In addition, your public library provides good sources for the latest technical information.

If you have done installation or handyman work in the past, you most likely own the needed tools. Even if you do not, the investment in basic tools is affordable. Another option: in the beginning you may want to rent any missing tools.

To establish competitive pricing for your work, you will have to learn the current basic rates negotiated in your area. Work deviations from the standard, as well as customized decorative installations, will be subject to surcharges. Such nonstandardized installations are not uncommon. In each instance calculate your fee carefully, for you must net a reasonable return on your labor and materials.

Determine whether your local licensing laws require you to take out liability insurance and be bonded. If so, comply with these laws and use this fact to your advantage in advertising.

Start your promotional efforts with some inexpensive classified newspaper ads, including the weekly suburban papers. Depending on location and size, appliance stores, department stores, and home centers may employ their own installer. Yet some may be interested in recommending your services to customers, so it doesn't hurt to pay them a visit. Also make personal contact with other good business sources: discount stores, building supply centers, and lighting specialty establishments. In addition to large appliances, most sell ceiling fans and air conditioners.

Suggested Reading

Gaddis, Ben. *How to Repair Kitchen Appliances.* Blue Ridge Summit, Pa.: Tab Books, 1983.

Home Repair Handbook. Sunset Books. Menlo Park, Calif.: Lane, 1985.

Meyerink, George. *Appliance Service Handbook.* 2d ed. Englewood Cliffs, N.J.: Prentice-Hall, 1988.

18

To Earn More Green, Care for People's Lawns

Are you one of those active outdoor people who swell with pride when neighbors point to your front lawn, exclaiming: "The grass is always greener on his side of the fence!"? More important, do your friends and neighbors frequently try to extract from you the secrets of your own lawn care?

More homeowners than ever are looking for professional lawn and yard care. Yet many are hesitant to patronize large maintenance companies. They dislike the impersonal approach of these "big boys," who screechily turn into the driveway with a sizable truck or two, then swarm noisily all over the property with rattling equipment. On the other hand, they prefer someone more dependable and accomplished than the boy or girl next door. They are looking for alternatives.

You can go after the business of these undecided homeowners, provided you really enjoy working diligently outdoors. Of course, you must have access to common yard tools and equipment, plus adequate transportation. In the beginning, renting tools and equipment is a sensible option.

As a small self-employed operator, you can start soliciting business in your own neighborhood. The service primarily consists of regular lawn mowing from spring to fall at a weekly or monthly based rate. Additionally, you can offer special services at established charges. They may include spring cleanup and leaf collection in the fall, as well as special lawn treatments or trimming of shrubs and hedges.

Take a close look at the rate schedule of larger companies and establish your own service charges accordingly. Consider offering services at discount rates if prospects are willing to give you a long-term commitment, which means contracting work from spring through fall or longer.

Because the work you do is obviously subject to public scrutiny, it must reflect neatness, dependability, and efficiency. Well-groomed front lawns and yards will speak for themselves. They will generate valuable word-of-mouth advertising.

Your promotional efforts should consist of a printed flyer outlining your services and a rate schedule that can be printed or photocopied. It's a good idea to distribute these materials personally in your neighborhood. Also display them on bulletin boards within the stores of nearby shopping centers. A few classified ads in the weekend edition of your local newspapers or neighborhood newsletters will be useful as well. All of this should get you off to a good start.

Precise work scheduling during the busy seasons is important. Perhaps your spouse or a family member can lend you a hand in setting up schedules for maximum efficiency. Keep the service volume manageable to prevent overbooking, which must be avoided, particularly during the height of the season. Reputable local professionals can assist you in setting up a suitable accounting system and in complying with existing small business requirements.

Once you're established in business, you may want to engage one or two dependable helpers (e.g., high school students) who may require supervision. After the first few profitable seasons, consider going on a well-deserved vacation. Also consider investing in a snowblower and adding snow removal to your business service. Keep in mind, however, the bigger the service equipment, the more difficulty you'll have in transporting it to and from your clients' property.

Suggested Reading

MacCaskey, Michael, et al., eds. *All About Lawns.* Rev. ed. San Francisco: Ortho Books, 1985.

Schery, Robert W. *A Perfect Lawn, the Easy Way.* New York: Collier-Macmillan, 1973.

Welcome, Robert. *How to Make Big Money Mowing Small Lawns.* San Marco, Calif.: Brick House, 1984.

19

Skilled in Graphic Displays? Try Picture Framing

Nowadays, walls of living quarters are covered with clever arrangements of decorative elements. It's stylish; it's trendy. These arrangements run the gamut from whimsical shadow boxes for miniatures to daring chrome-framed contemporary artworks to life-size medieval brass rubbings under plexiglass protection. The variety is exciting and limitless.

If you are a meticulous, imaginative craftsperson with a sharp eye for effective display of graphics, picture framing may appeal to you as an income-producing and challenging business. With the explosion in popularity of home and office decorating, plus the surge of crafts, the need for customized display framing or casing has never been greater. Simple picture framing without individualized decorative touch is out—at least for the time being.

Although many cities now have well-equipped do-it-yourself framing workshops, there is always room for another creative custom framer. Numerous homemakers accessorize their home on a year-round basis. Yet they are too busy or lack confidence and imagination to get personally involved in tedious do-it-yourself framing. This large market of prospective customers needs to be tapped.

To sharpen your knowledge of picture framing, contact your public library—which carries numerous books on the subject—and consult art journals. Then visit your local museum(s) and take time to study the fine art of framing. Commercial art galleries will enlighten you on the latest framing materials and techniques. Carefully observe the newest trends in the modern art world. Framers' shops, usually stacked to the ceiling with posters and prints, also abound, but they cater primarily to those customers whose needs don't exceed the framing of posters, prints, diplomas, and office art. It is mandatory for anyone in the trade to be familiar with the total range of framing applications.

When visiting commercial establishments, investigate the prices charged for material and labor, and let your findings be the guide in setting up your own fee schedule. For wholesale supply sources, consult your local Yellow Pages.

You can improve your chances of getting your business off to a smooth start by creating a number of different types of graphic displays and having them photographed. Incorporate the most attractive ones into your promotional portfolio, and enhance your circular with sketches of some unusual creations. Attach your circular to bulletin boards of supermarkets, shopping malls, and apartment buildings. Then call personally on stores and studios that sell antiques, art, and/or photography, and which are not commercially involved in on-the-premise framing. Print shops may also be willing to recommend you to their customers. This is a start in the right direction to gradually build a loyal contractor and customer base. After you have gained confidence and experience, pay a personal visit with your promotional material to interior decorators and design studios in your area. They should be in a position to steer plenty of custom framing jobs in your direction.

Finally, a custom framer must secure an adequate workplace. A self-built or secondhand work station and tools, if not available to you now, will become your major investment. Be certain to comply with your local zoning laws and state and community licensing and tax requirements. Established local professionals can counsel you on your community's business regulations.

Suggested Reading

Burnett, Lawrence. *Picture Framer's Handbook.* New York: Crown, 1973.

Hyder, Max. *Matting, Mounting, and Framing Art.* New York: Watson-Guptill, 1986.

Newman, Thelma. *The Framer's Book: Contemporary Designs with Traditional and Modern Methods and Materials.* New York: Crown, 1974.

20

‖‖‖➡ ⬅‖‖‖

Mr. and Ms. Fix-It: For Bicycle and Toy Repairs, Your Neighborhood Needs You

Are your friends and neighbors addressing you as Mr. or Ms. Fix-It? Great! Seize the opportunity and cash in on your talents. The rewards will be threefold: working in a field you enjoy, taking personal satisfaction in helping your neighbors, and bringing home a good cash income.

In spite of a rapidly advancing technology, breakdowns of basic home conveniences are not going to be eliminated in the foreseeable future. As any homeowner can confirm, there always will be leaking faucets, clogged drains, groaning garbage disposals, nonflushing toilets, dripping water heaters, and malfunctioning furnaces. An accomplished *Mr. or Ms. Fix-It* knows how to quickly diagnose these problems and to expeditiously perform minor household repairs.

Have you performed home repair work in the past? Most likely you own the tools necessary to complete such jobs. If not, see the books recommended at the end of this chapter for guidance on what tools to buy or rent. The books also give tips on work safety.

To spread the word about your service, have a flyer prepared and printed at a quick print shop. Distribute the material in residential areas and home-care centers, real estate agencies, and the Welcome Wagon organization. Then tack the flyer to bulletin boards of food markets, shopping malls, and churches. Soon you can count on new business and referrals from satisfied customers.

And then there are *bicycle repairs*. It's a field you may want to explore if you have done this type of work in the past, perhaps as a hobby. In addition to reading the two technical sources listed at the end of this chapter, you may want to subscribe to the *Bicycle Business Journal*, Box 1570, 1940 Wenneca, Fort Worth, TX 76101. You can even go to bicycle repair school. If interested, send $1 for a how-to-start information kit to Bicycle Repair of America, P.O. Box 24106, Minneapolis, MN 55424.

Unless you live in a large inner-city area, you are aware of the countless adults' and children's bicycles of all makes and styles found in every neighborhood. In addition, hundreds of families own stationary exercise bikes. To go after all this potential business, you must map out a promotional strategy. Place some inexpensive classified ads in your weekly neighborhood papers or in shoppers' bulletins. Also offer your services to bicycle, fitness, and youth clubs. Then concentrate your distribution of circulars on residential neighborhoods and supermarkets. Try to approach school administrators to make your service available to their bicycling pupils. Once you feel confident about your repair skills, contact stores that sell bicycles, including chain and discount stores. Some of them might be willing to subcontract repair work or to refer their customers to you.

Most bike problems can be repaired at the customer's home. Others may have to be taken to your home workshop. Therefore, a spacious transportation vehicle is required.

Now you have become well established in the bicycle repair trade! But what are you going to do during the slow winter months? What about taking advantage of the cash-on-the-spot opportunity of setting up an *assembly service* from late November to January, or longer? You can even expand the service into *toy repair*. No statistics are available, but when January comes, the amount of toys in need of repair seems staggering.

Consumer goods that need assembling range from toys and decorative occasional pieces to exercise equipment. To keep the shipping costs down and the merchandise competitive, more and more manufacturers are producing unassembled gift items each year. Yet many consumers have neither the time nor the technical understanding—not to mention the patience—to put this merchandise into workable condition in time for the holidays. As early as November each year, you can pick up additional work from small and medium-sized retail stores. Numerous retail establishments are compelled to look for outside help to assemble merchandise arriving for floor displays.

If you do bicycle repair in addition to this seasonal work, you can publicize all your services on the same circular. Or have a five-by-seven-inch flyer printed in a bold color and emphasize your speciality: dependable assembly and toy repair service.

A local certified public accountant can design an appropriate recordkeeping system for your service. He or she will also advise you on existing small business requirements.

Suggested Reading

Basic Home Repairs. Do-It-Yourself Library. Sunset Books. Menlo Park, Calif.: Lane, 1985.

Basic Home Wiring. Do-It-Yourself Library. Sunset Books. Menlo Park, Calif.: Lane, 1987.

Basic Plumbing. Do-It-Yourself Library. Sunset Books. Menlo Park, Calif.: Lane, 1975.

Cuthbertson, Tom. *Anybody's Bike Book.* Berkeley, Calif.: Ten Speed Press, 1984.

Van der Plas, Rob. *The Bicycle Repair Book.* San Francisco: Bicycle Books, 1985.

Waugh, Andrew. *The Complete How-to-Fix-It Book.* New York: Bonanza Books, 1974.

21

Is Home Remodeling Your Business? Become a Consultant

Just about everyone has heard about the do-it-yourself enthusiast on the next block down the street who began remodeling his home, only to end up with a new floor of the kitchen extension caving in. Or remember the fellow whose new customized stained glass windows were too large, and he built a new addition to the house just to use them? For both, the experience was costly, to say the least.

Perhaps you have worked for a building contractor or a building material enterprise, or you may have had your own business remodeling and selling older homes. Here is an excellent chance to capitalize on your experience. With an all-around knowledge of the remodeling trade and a healthy dose of self-confidence, you can become a consultant to those homeowners who plan to do their own home renovating. At the outset of any home-improvement project, do-it-yourself homeowners are faced with difficult technical decision making. As a result, the initial enthusiasm for the project begins to wane quickly, and these homeowners start looking around for some affordable professional assistance.

Individuals who have gone into this type of consulting business in recent years attest to a steadily growing demand for their service. Take, for example, the experiences of two mature individuals turned remodeling consultants. Both had eased into this new service by accident. Neighbors and acquaintances had besieged them for technical advice. And word about their professional know-how began to spread. With plenty of time on their hands, both decided to embark on a financially rewarding retirement career.

As you are well aware, each homeowner's plans and requirements are different. Even a simple-looking job can involve a multitude of decisions. How much material should be ordered? What grade of materials should be selected? (Remember, when ordering prefabricated or customized parts, that they are not returnable.) Does the purchased blueprint fit the planned renovation or are revisions necessary? What is the first step to be taken? What must be torn down and what can be saved or reused? Should part of the work be subcontracted?

Homeowners also need to know: Do invited contractor bids really cover all the work they are expected to do? Are any structural problems anticipated? Will the remodeling job affect the utilities? Will the planned work comply with the local building code?

These are the concerns with which a knowledgeable remodeling consultant will be confronted. He or she recommends, advises, and supervises. During conversations with three consultants, they emphasized that in many cases, using a consultant adds up to substantial savings for the homeowner. They noted that a more professional-looking finished job leads to an enhancement of property values.

When questioned about remuneration, the consultants gave various answers. They implied that the type of remodeling job largely determines the compensation. Service fee and the specific consultation areas are best detailed in a simple contract. In case of a limited assignment, the charge consists of a percentage of the total amount spent on materials, usually between 15 and 25 percent. Charges for more comprehensive assignments are frequently based on an hourly rate. As with any other new service, these rates should be investigated locally.

A few consultants admitted that, in the beginning, they shortchanged themselves by not charging enough to adequately cover their efforts. Therefore, estimate carefully the time you expect to spend on each job. And with the assistance of established local professionals, examine and comply with your community's licensing, tax, and bonding requirements for this consulting business.

Start your promotional efforts with several classified ads in your local daily and weekly newspapers. Furthermore, try to place some ads in in-house organs of large local businesses and utility companies. Or obtain permission to tack business cards or flyers on their bulletin boards. The printed flyer should also be posted on bulletin boards of local credit union offices and distributed at spring and fall home-remodeling fairs and exhibits at area shopping malls. These are excellent opportunities to meet prospective clients. In addition, talk to managers of building supply stores, lumberyards, hardware and surplus stores. Leave your business card with them and request that they give your name to customers looking for a remodeling consultant. In time, satisfied clients will spread the word about your service in neighborhoods, service clubs, and corporations.

Suggested Reading

Home Remodeling. Sunset Books. Menlo Park, Calif.:
Lane, 1987.

Lant, Jeffrey L. *The Consultant's Kit.* 2d ed. Cambridge,
Mass.: JLA Publications, 1981.

Ortho's Home Improvement Encyclopedia. San
Francisco: Ortho Books, 1985.

22

Home Inspector: Every Home Buyer Needs One

Has the extensive home-building business been your
domain? Perhaps you have been a building inspector on
the state, county, or municipality level. Or you may
have an engineering, architectural, or technical degree
and years of experience in the construction field. If so,
consider establishing a home inspection service. It is
stimulating work which can produce a handsome income.

For the majority of people the purchase of a home is
the single largest purchase they will ever make. Yet it
happens again and again—the love-at-first-sight home
turns unexpectedly into a nightmare for the new buyer.
Many times, home defects and hazards are not uncovered until after the new owner has settled into the newly
purchased home. As a home inspector, you become a

valuable, trusted impartial consultant to local home buyers, not only giving them peace of mind but sometimes saving them thousands of dollars in costly repairs.

Right after the buyer's offer has been accepted by the home seller, and before the final sales closing, the real estate agent frequently lends a hand in arranging a time when the home inspector can go through the seller's home. It's noteworthy, though, that it is up to the home buyer to seek legal counsel or the real estate agent's advice on whether to include a protective clause in the home purchase agreement to the effect that the sale is contingent on allowing an inspection.

When seeking an inspection, the home buyer starts by contacting various independent local home inspectors to obtain a free inspection estimate. Generally, the home buyer selects the most suitable home inspector after examining the bidder's estimate, references, credentials, and his or her membership in a professional association. Once the buyer has signed the home inspector's contract, the professional is ready to begin the work he or she has been hired to do.

The inspector conducts a thorough, impartial analysis of the property's condition and summarizes the findings in a comprehensive, yet easy-to-understand, client inspection report. An exhaustive inspection focuses on everything from the foundation and basement, to the heating, cooling, plumbing, and electrical systems, to walls, floors, windows, built-in appliances, insulation, waterspouts, roof, as well as exterior drainage and landscaping.

Because housing costs vary geographically, so do inspection fees. Time, size, and complexity of the individual job have a bearing on the fee schedule. Therefore, investigate the going rates for professional services in your own or neighboring community.

A few classified ads in the real estate section of your local daily newspaper(s) and weekly suburban newsletter are in order. Then place some ads in the home buyer guide/news of larger local banks. You should also list your service as soon as possible in your local Yellow Pages.

A home inspector's impartiality is paramount in any home examination. Therefore, local real estate brokers should not be included in any promotional campaign where even a hint of conflict of interest exists.

As always, carefully examine the local licensing, tax, bonding, and liability requirements and with the assistance of an established local professional team (attorney, accountant, insurance professional), form your own consulting service.

If you want to explore the option of buying a franchise, you can choose from several national franchisers. Appendix B provides details on how to order the latest directory of franchising organizations. For information on the field of home inspection, contact the American Society of Home Inspectors, 3299 K Street NW, 7th Floor, Washington, DC 20007; (202) 842-3096. This society of professionals has developed inspection guidelines and a professional code of ethics, and offers a variety of publications in the field. A second trade group is the National Association of Home Inspectors, 5775 Wayzata Boulevard, Minneapolis, MN 55416; (800) 448-3942. This organization makes available liability insurance to trade members.

Home Inspections Are on the Rise

Is the home inspection market already over-crowded? John Simler, owner of Homescan Inspection Service, Inc., doesn't think so, and his impressive business record proves it. With a background in architecture and the building inspection field, John, thirtyish and people-oriented, formed his own independent, nonfranchised consulting business over six years ago. From modest beginnings in the first year, this home inspector gradually expanded his service business over a three-county area from which he draws considerable repeat business. Now, with more than 600 home inspections per year, John's home-based computer-operated one-person service has reached its full capacity. This home inspector seems to thoroughly enjoy his flourishing service activities, notwithstanding his work load, plus paperwork, which he efficiently streamlined. Interested in starting a home inspection service? John recommends that your first step should be to contact the American Society of Home Inspectors in Washington, D.C. (see Appendix A for the address and phone number).

Suggested Reading

Scaduto, Joseph V. *What's It Worth? A Home Inspection and Appraisal Manual.* Blue Ridge Summit, Pa.: Tab Books, 1985.

23

Printing Is Big Business: Brokers Are Welcome

Do you thoroughly enjoy interacting with people and speaking to office managers, purchasing agents, or business proprietors? And is your past sales record a good one? Then nothing stands in your way to an exciting part-time or full-time activity as a printing broker or representative.

Small and medium-sized businesses, health-care institutions, professional offices, restaurants, and numerous civic organizations and church offices need a great variety of printed materials. These include stationery, accounting or production forms, scores of internal management and computer forms, plus countless printed advertising materials.

Simple enough to order, you think? By no means. Purchasing agents and office managers must frequently deal with four or more different salespersons, each representing a different printing source. It would be far easier for businesses to order their printed materials through one prime channel. And you can help! Represent a group of reputable local printing establishments that together cover the full range of customer requirements.

Start by perusing the listings of specialized printers in the Yellow Pages. Note that some printers specialize in quality color processes, layout and design, catalog and publication printing. Others are sources of business and computer forms, labels, stationery, and everything from newsletters to volume runs of circulars. Finally, there are numerous quick printers. Begin the selection process by contacting two to three firms in each category and by inquiring about their sales programs and production capacities. Some may already have a well-established sales network, while others may be willing to give you a chance by offering you a specific sales territory. Negotiate a representation agreement and fair commission rate only with firms you feel comfortable with. The printers have nothing to lose but everything to gain. Make sure you end up with a solid and diverse base of printers so you can take care of any printing job your clients might have.

You can also serve as a broker for one of the large, nationally known, competitive printing companies. To gain access to these enterprises, you will have to screen printing trade magazines, available at your local public library. These magazines carry ads that invite readers to inquire about broker opportunities and to request a free sample kit. The kit contains a variety of printing samples and sets of forms to complete any sales transaction. The samples are designed to appeal to the widest range of businesses. Take advantage of as many free offers as possible.

All offers for work should be carefully examined. Check each company's credibility and dependability with your local Better Business Bureau and in credit rating directories. Select only those firms that offer good sales commissions and whose business credentials are impeccable.

Equipped with your sample kit, you can now call on the range of businesses as listed above. Quality workmanship and competitive pricing will open the door to many prospective business customers. They will welcome dealing with only one broker instead of several for all their diverse printing needs.

Following the printing company's order-taking instructions, you will have to collect from each new customer a downpayment on his/her first order. The percentage will vary, but should be in the 20 to 35 percent range. After the printing house receives your customer's order, it will handle all ensuing order processing including billing.

Making follow-up customer calls and helping customers handle any possible snags are essential activities. You want to keep your customers satisfied.

Establish early in your planning your own business references. The customer who entrusts you with his/her downpayment check deserves every consideration. Support your sales efforts with your own well-executed printed business cards and stationery from the firm(s) you will represent. They are your most effective advertising.

Many communities now feature a concentration of small businesses in malls, industrial parks with numerous small manufacturing outlets, and commercial building complexes with scores of professional offices. Visiting such locations will greatly simplify your sales efforts. Cultivate your customers with excellent service. In return, they'll give you lucrative repeat business.

Before starting any serious planning, familiarize yourself with your community's licensing, sales tax, and liability laws.

24

||||➡   ⬅||||

Organize a Referral Service Everyone Needs

We can all relate to Sheila W.'s nasty plumbing emergency. Water flooded her basement not long after she had moved into her home. Because she was new in the area and had not established contacts with service firms, she had to run for the Yellow Pages, only to face pages of listings of unknown service companies. Hurriedly, she dialed the telephone number of the company topping the first column. Then came the familiar recording: "This number has been disconnected!"

Relax! There is now a better way to quickly find a competent service person. What about being the first in your immediate area to offer a useful referral service for home repairs? Yes, a system designed to quickly and efficiently bring together the service-hunting consumer with a reputable local service business. In good and in bad economic times, now and then every home is in dire need of dependable repair and maintenance service.

Peter Vaughn, an energetic former shop maintenance supervisor, had heard through a friend in Florida about various types of service-oriented businesses. "Bringing the customer and the service business together appealed to me," he said, so he set up his own successful referral service.

The first step in starting your business: draft a strategy plan. Clearly define the two groups of people you wish to bring together by telephone. When service inquiries come your way, you'll furnish, free-of-charge, three choices of and information on local tradespeople and service firms. The remuneration for this finder service is a commission paid on each actual business transaction by the service firm.

The next step is to list the basic services you wish to represent. Include appliance, furnace, and air-conditioning repair firms; electricians and plumbing and roofing contractors; chimney sweepers; businesses that handle pest control, fire and water damage, TV, radio, and VCR repair, as well as other electronic equipment services. Additional key services are house and office cleaning, window washing, drapery, upholstery, and carpet cleaning. Equally important is the remodeling field: house painting, plastering, wallpaper hanging, carpentry services, bricklaying, installation of flooring and insulation, and masonry work. The outdoor services should cover lawn maintenance, snow removal, concrete work, gutter cleaning. Expand your service listings as business grows. Contact at least five representatives from each selected service group.

Present a questionnaire to each tentatively selected firm. Each service firm or tradesperson must furnish precise information which is later passed on to the inquiring consumer. Sample questions that should be asked: Number of years in business? Is the firm licensed, insured, bonded? Does it furnish free estimates and grant senior citizens' discount? What are the names and phone numbers of business references? Compiling all this information will be a time-consuming task, even if you personally know many of your local service businesses. But the information will form an essential database for your business file system.

Be certain to select only reliable and reputable firms and individuals. They should be listed in the Yellow Pages and in local business directories. Also check them out with your chamber of commerce, the Small Business Administration, and the local Better Business Bureau.

You should have no problems registering desirable businesses. Service companies recognize the advantages of working with a service of this kind. The association undoubtedly stimulates business and frequently compensates for seasonal slumps. The no-investment aspect—commission payment upon completion of the work—plus the free publicity are excellent selling points. A 5 to 10 percent commission on each completed service transaction is generally accepted.

It is important to find the right name for your referral service. If you have trouble coming up with a catchy name, ask the assistance of friends and family members. Two names you might consider are Direct-Line to Top Services and Service Direct-Line.

Your start-up money should cover the services of a reputable local accountant (in setting up a simple accounting system that will let you monitor the commission due to you by the service providers), the purchases of a telephone answering machine and file system, as well as costs for the extensive research and the marketing campaign. Depending on your professional background, the latter can be done with or without the assistance of a competent advertising agency.

It's essential that your service name gets maximum exposure. Personally distribute printed circulars to stores that sell products requiring service by the trades you will represent. Also visit tenants of apartment buildings, customers of moving companies, truck rental firms, and stores that cater to the remodeling businesses. Don't overlook building supply centers, garden supply stores, as well as equipment and rental outlets. Additionally, have a flyer inserted in Welcome Wagon literature. At the time you launch your service, place a few classified ads in local daily newspapers, weekly suburban papers, shoppers' bulletins. The same applies to real estate agents' newsletters to new home buyers and bank publications that also target the homeowners' and buyers' markets. Furthermore, try to get the attention of the business or city editor of your local newspaper(s). Most of them will consent to run a profile on the owner of a new community-oriented service.

Alternatives to the described basic, community-service approach are the referral services as they exist in larger metropolitan areas. Many of these services span several counties, and their listings can run the gamut from adult day care to zipper repair. They may also include professional services, such as those of accountants, attorneys, tax consultants, health-care professionals, and designers.

A strong background in business or marketing is the prerequisite for such a venture. It requires a considerably higher investment in research, electronic equipment, and marketing strategy. Use of a computer and customized software is mandatory. Because this type of referral service makes great demands on the owner's energy and financial resources, it is not for everyone.

The usual source of revenues for the owner of an extended referral service is the registration/listing network fee, which service companies, tradespeople, and professionals pay periodically. In some instances, a combination of commission and listing fee is used instead.

Many municipalities do not require licensing for a referral service. However, be sure to consult a competent attorney and insurance professional for advice on how to comply with community ordinances, state tax, and liability coverage requirements.

25

Professional Drafting: Selling a Specialized Skill

Let's assume, until recently, you have been associated with the drafting profession, perhaps as an instructor or as an employed draftsperson. And are you now looking for an opportunity to turn your expertise into cash? Here is the answer—you can develop a part-time activity in a full-fledged service business without sitting behind a drafting table.

Any city with a healthy blend of manufacturing and

interactive professional and trade enterprises holds promise to support a home-based drafting service. The core of such business is a small, yet expandable, pool of qualified and reliable free-lance draftspersons. In your capacity as go-between of the supply and demand sectors, you will solicit drafting assignments from professional, commercial, and industrial clients. In turn, you will farm out the work to the best-suited draftsperson from your established work pool.

To recruit suitable free-lance draftspeople, start by running a few classified ads in your local newspapers. Other sources will be art and drafting supply stores, technical institutions and colleges in your area, and, if available, the local chapter of the American Design Drafting Association.

Extend your search to local printing and reproduction establishments that serve building contractors, architects, and engineering firms. Generally, proprietors of these companies have frequent contacts with drafting personnel. Also, make good use of your past professional connections.

The next step is to carefully examine the recruits' workmanship and work habits. Incorporate your observations and judgments into a handy, factual subcontractor file. The emphasis should be on recording each subcontractor's field of specialization. Your future reputation and business success will hinge on the degree to which you will capitalize on your subcontractors' proficiency.

As a precautionary measure, keep the names of your free-lancers confidential. They should not be divulged to clients. On the other hand, the client's name cannot always be kept from the contracted draftsperson due to labeled drafting assignments. But some assignment coding may become necessary. Use discretion, be flexible, and avoid direct contact between your clientele and the contracted work force.

A listing of prospective clients can be compiled from your library's commercial directories. Begin with professional offices such as architectural, engineering, and consulting firms, and patent attorneys, all of which farm out drafting work on a regular basis. Don't rule out work from local, county, and state government agencies.

Seasonal drafting work is needed by a variety of building contractors: manufacturers in general, and the large number of small machine shops in particular. The latter include tool and die makers, injection molders, die casters, machine builders, and repair shops.

Research the current drafting rates in your area before setting up your own fee schedule. This will also give you a good foundation for negotiating rates with your free-lancers. Carefully calculate the total expenses before finalizing charges to clients. The fee should reflect an adequate compensation for your managerial input.

Your new service promotion can be launched by personally calling on the various commercial and professional groups listed above. Visits should be supported by well-prepared circulars that outline your services. If necessary, supplement your personal calls with some weekend classified advertisements in your daily newspapers and local commercial publications. A listing in the Yellow Pages is also recommended.

Have reputable local professionals (attorney, accountant, insurance professional) advise you on all service-related regulations. And finally, if you need to update your drafting know-how, take out one or more of the extensive professional publications on the subject available at your public library.

A Team of Two Is Successfully Serving Professionals

Less than a year after establishing Paradise Engineering and Detailing, Inc., co-owner Karl P. Schmidt moved his home-based engineering and detailing service into larger rented quarters. An early indicator of impending success? With a background in the professional drafting business and in marketing, Karl appears well qualified for operating an independent service venture. Yet giving up secure employment and striking out on your own means sparring with unforeseen risks. The two partners immediately offered their drafting and detailing service mainly to an industrial-professional clientele. It has been only two years since the opening day, but thanks to sensible business planning, counseling from SCORE, and broadening their client base, the service company is now well positioned within an economically active area that spans several counties. Words of advice to would-be entrepreneurs: plan your expansion carefully and be mindful of your financial reserves.

Part III

Personalized Miniservices for a Team, Partners, or Solo

26

║║║➤ ◄║║║

Plant Leasing: An Ideal Venture for Houseplant Growers

A couple experienced in houseplant care and living in their own home; a congenial group of two or three men or women friends regularly sharing their love for indoor greenery—what do they have in common? Either would make an excellent team for a new type of service business venture, called plant leasing.

Imagine, if you will, a climatically conditioned Florida room filled with a plethora of potted houseplants. Multiplied by reflection in the mirrored rear walls are opulent hanging baskets of luxuriant ferns, robost peperomias, and prolific picturatums (spider plants). Decoratively positioned and cleverly mixed for contrast on the tile floor and tiered display stands are the lush and variegated foliage of Chinese bamboo, Schefflera, Dracaena, Dieffenbachia, and thick-leaved rubber plants. This is certainly a splendid setting for a newly opened plant-leasing and -care service. But even a less impressive backdrop will serve you well in an indoor plant leasing service.

Let's take a look at the growing demand for rented indoor plants. First, there are numerous specialty stores and boutiques, including retail stores of the furniture and home-decorating trade that favor showing off lush foliage as a backdrop for their decorative display settings. Next are the professional offices with waiting areas or lobbies: offices of physicians, dentists, hospitals, other health-care providers, law firms, insurance agencies, brokerage firms, banks, real estate brokers, travel and advertising agencies. In addition, numerous small and large corporate offices, encouraged by their interior decorators, have joined the ranks of live indoor "plantscape" enthusiasts. The majority of businesses actually prefer the leasing arrangement to ownership of indoor plants, primarily because it relieves their employees of the responsibility of tricky plant care.

Prior to any investment, explore the following: How many services operate in your community? What are their current leasing rates? Is there a prospective clientele right in your neighborhood? Does your current dwelling provide enough room for a small display and work area? Do you have ample car space to move large plants? What about a strong-bodied person to assist in pickups and deliveries? If you decide to go into this business, invest in some professional plant-care publications and in a number of basic sources (see the listing at the end of Chapter 11).

You'll also need to exercise good judgment in selecting first-rate, healthy plants at reputable wholesale sources. Research this phase carefully; study current trends and survey the preferences of prospective clients. Be sure to stay within your start-up budget.

Aside from providing the particular plants desired by clients, you must reach an agreement with them on plant positioning. Rarely are two client settings exactly alike; variables include size of display area, lighting and climatic conditions, as well as proximity to traffic patterns.

The minimum period for plant leasing should be at least six months. To establish monthly leasing fee scales, several factors must be taken into account: the plant's original purchase price, the cost of plant maintenance and transportation, and the cost of replacing the plant in case of damage or disease. Also estimate the inventory of maintenance products: plant food, fertilizer, potting soil. The array of decorative articles—containers, rocks, hangers—must be taken into account as well. For all your needs, use wholesale buying sources.

Although you will not be operating a retail business, you do need to comply with your area's zoning ordinance, as well as licensing and tax regulations. Also, consult a reputable insurance professional about required liability coverage.

It's a good idea to start your business with not more than five to ten clients. Recruiting these clients should prove neither costly nor difficult. With business card, printed circular, and blank contract form in hand, call

PLANT LEASING
800-1110
Interior Landscaping
Affordable Maintenance
Programs
Live and Artificial
"LEASE IT FROM
HENRY AND JANE"

on professional offices with waiting rooms and decorative lobbies. After gaining experience in the new trade, you may want to contact developers of office buildings and managers of office furniture supply houses to gain access to their new tenants and customers, respectively. Giving superior service will put you several steps ahead of any competitor.

If you so desire, your plant rental service can be gradually developed into a profitable retailing business. An effective long-range business plan is essential to this endeavor.

27

Gourmet Chefs and Other Cooks: Taste These Possibilities

Gourmet catering, party-fare cooking—is this the kind of business you would love to be in? Are you an undiscovered, but skilled, cook? Well, if your friends and relatives rave about your cooking, and if you can recruit one or more of them to go into partnership with you, nothing should keep you from realizing this dream!

Once the fond wish of many obscure yet capable cooks, party planning for adults or children, gourmet catering, or setting up a home cooking school has now become a reality for once timid but talented creators of culinary masterpieces. Many have discovered multiple profitable opportunities. They have resolutely gone public with their talents and happily bank their rewards every week. Some of the more common catering businesses listed below may appeal to you.

Caterers of specialty foods, such as cookies, cakes, breads (or jams, sauces, dressings), head the listing. They concentrate on supplying small eateries, cafeterias, snack bars, luncheonettes, and country inns. Their products require some distinction from the supermarket variety and need to be market-tested, promoted, and to display recognizable labeling.

Wedding cake, special occasion pastry and dessert caterers primarily seek out the neighborhood consumer market. Such a venture can be expanded by contacting wedding consultants as well as the wedding supplies and hall rental trades.

Casserole dishes during the winter season, and picnic lunches during the rest of the year, are being regularly catered to senior citizens' centers, retirement clubs, and any group that holds monthly social gatherings. In addition, business can be generated through women's and men's clubs, church congregations, civic organizations. All are interested in *catered party food* for their informal get-togethers.

Catered box lunches have also become fashionable with cultural and educational institutions for their seasonal outdoor lectures, concerts, art showings, and fairs. Some *box-lunch caterers* rely on daily phone-in orders, as well as on-the-spot trade to office and factory workers.

Yet greater publicity is generally given to the *gourmet food caterers* whose businesses are slated not only to socially prominent hosts and hostesses, but also to upscale social affairs. In this particular line, the successful caterer displays flexibility and easily adapts to ever-changing food trends.

Interested Gourmet Cooks, Please Listen!
From professionally performing and teaching music to successfully creating acclaimed culinary treats has been a long, uphill effort for Tracy Woll. Ten years after forming up-scale Intimate Affairs Caterers in Akron, Ohio, with her husband as business partner, the genial and energetic entrepreneur was named "Caterer of the Year" by *Catering Today* magazine, with Julia Child presenting the magazine's award to the winner. Congratulations, Tracy! For six years the caterer operated out of her home. Now, in larger commercial quarters, a full- and part-time staff of fine professionals support the prize-winning caterer in her prospering enterprise. Newcomers to the catering field take note: Tracy practices what she teaches—measured growth means healthy growth.

The party-catering field will prove rewarding to those who can add creative ideas and touches to their service. A caterer often starts out orchestrating children's parties. Besides food, the caterer team takes care of anything ranging from invitations and decorations to entertainment and prizes. With a flair for originality, *children and adult theme parties* can be elevated to a financially rewarding specialty business with little competition.

The key to financial success in the catering business is a well-functioning, efficient team of at least two persons. And they must excel in courtesy, dependabilty, and professionalism. Likewise, bulk food purchases of top-notch ingredients are mandatory. Catered food must not only meet quality standards but also be tasty and attractive. Because caterers are subject to municipal health department inspections, the food must be prepared in sanitary surroundings.

An imaginative variation on the catering business is to serve as *caterer/teacher at a cooking party*. It's particularly appealing to many persons because it requires little investment and can easily be managed by either one or two persons. Yet it differs distinctly from traditional home cooking schools, which are now mushrooming throughout the country. Why not test this idea in your community?

The caterer/teacher works with locally known hosts and hostesses, who graciously arrange a party of interested participants in the latter's home kitchen. For example, in a midwestern city, Victoria Simmons, a vivacious fortyish gourmet cook, supplies all major ingredients for the party event. She demonstrates in detail the preparation of a full-course meal to the party guests. Being a knowledgeable and resourceful cook, Victoria prepares theme lessons that range from Scandinavian cooking to French cuisine, from light upscale meals to speedy party fare and everything in between.

Every party participant pays a per-person share of the prearranged total host fee. Depending on the individual circumstances, the per-person share generally amounts to anywhere from $15 to $20. The participants' reward is twofold: working knowledge of first-rate cuisine, plus a superb full-course meal.

The teacher should see to it that the occasion is not all hard work. By adopting a light attitude and making sure that participants have fun, he or she can earn new bookings on the spot, saving valuable advertising dollars.

And what about the growing popularity of *cooking schools and classes*? They are profiled in Chapter 36.

If you are interested in pursuing one of the described catering services, first inquire about your local zoning, licensing, food inspection, and tax laws. Then engage established local professionals (attorney, accountant, insurance professional) to organize your new service business.

Suggested Reading

Blanchard, Marjorie P. *Cater from Your Kitchen*. Indianapolis: Bobbs-Merrill, 1981.

Howard, Alice. *Turn Your Kitchen into a Goldmine*. New York: Harper and Row, 1981.

Lawrence, Elizabeth. *The Complete Caterer*. Garden City, N.Y.: Doubleday, 1988.

Shown, Janet. *Freelance Foodcrafting*. Boulder, Colo.: Live Oak, 1983.

28

If You Know Your Hometown Well, Organizing Tours May Be for You

Let's bring your city into sharp focus. Does it have a distinct cultural and environmental heritage? Is tourism on the rise and being publicly promoted? How many sightseeing tour operators exist in your community? None? One? Your local chamber of commerce, area development board, or convention bureau will gladly furnish desired information.

Successful tour conducting requires a special type of partnership. Partners must be able to communicate effectively with each other and have excellent organizational skills. A husband and wife, or two or three resourceful friends, can pool their experiences and interests to establish a fascinating part-time business.

Nowadays a variety of tour programs are marketed in our cities. The most common ones are local sightseeing tours. Depending on the availability of local points of interest, these can range from one and a half hours to a full day. Tours can be restricted to local historical sites, which are found in most communities and counties. An excellent information source for the coordination of such tours is your local historical society.

Walking tours can be offered to local groups of all ages. They can be built around special urban or suburban points of interest. Consider providing a walking tour at one of your metropolitan parks. And what about offering tours of area mansions that are open to the public? Or tours to visit the area's outstanding architectural structures, or its art museums and technology/science exhibitions? How about a tour of private art galleries, topped off with a luncheon in a first-rate or theme restaurant?

Regardless of the tour's theme, you can gain the competitive edge through creative thinking, leading to new or unique touches in tour conducting. Keep the presentation lively, occasionally injecting humorous commentary. Don't rush the tourists! Allow time for questioning, and where appropriate, plan time for a shopping stop, coffee break, or even a luncheon rest. By all means, first test each developed tour program by inviting family members and friends and their candid comments. If necessary, make changes.

Transportation, an important factor in the touring business, will have to be chartered—unless you happen to own a van with comfortable passenger seating and, in addition, are a seasoned driver with a chauffeur license.

Bus chartering should be available in your own or neighboring city. Pretour sign-ups are mandatory, to determine the size of the vehicle and to make all necessary reservations.

When calculating tour fees, take into account the vehicle lease, driver's cost, additional insurance, gasoline mileage, and any admission fees and food cost. You must net a reasonable compensation for your work. To stay competitive, compare your estimate with other area tour charges.

Your promotional expenditures should primarily be channeled into a well-executed folder, plus circular and classified advertising. Distribution points for your promotional material should be downtown hotels, suburban motels, inns, and local transportation terminals (air, rail, and bus). Besides introducing your services to your local chamber of commerce and trade development organizations, distribute your printed material at convention facilities and at reputable restaurants that draw nonresident patrons. Others that tend to generate a constant flow of out-of-town visitors are corporations, manufacturing plants, large local employers, and educational institutions. Also place ads on a regular basis in any publication that caters to the local tourist trade.

In some communities the touring business may be subject to special regulations. Study your area's licensing, bonding, and tax laws. Have reputable local professionals, such as attorney, accountant, insurance professional, counsel you on your community's requirements.

29

||||➤ ◀||||

Big City Resident: Conventioneers' Spouses Need Your Service

No doubt about it, living in a big city has its advantages. Do you live in or near a metropolitan or resort area with brisk convention traffic? If you do, take a close look at a novel money-making service idea introduced during the past decade by enterprising men and women. It might be just the type of new stimulating activity you have been waiting for.

Those people who accompany their spouses to conventions frequently become bored while their mates are busy with drawn-out meetings. Not everyone has the desire to fetch a taxi and head for the leading department store or suburban shopping malls. Now conventioneers' spouses have the option of taking attractive specialized area tours tailor-made for them.

There is no limit to the subjects that can be developed into appealing tour programs. Organize tours to historical sites or to rehabilitated age-old residential or shopping/open market districts; to various types of museums (art, technology and science, nature and history); to botanical gardens; to exceptional educational institutions and their exhibitions; to fascinating architectural structures or to mansions open to the public. Let's add trips to showrooms of fashion establishments; to interior design centers; to unique jewelry crafters; to art and craft galleries; to fine restaurants for luncheons or teas; to brand-name factory-outlet stores.

First, ferret out the points of interest in your greater metropolitan area. Carefully record your discoveries. Then develop a staple of standard tours, and introduce a few original themes, to make your tour service attractive and competitive.

A well-functioning, congenial team of two or three is vital to the success of the service. Excellent local information sources for the development of tour services are your chamber of commerce, convention center, area trade developing organizations, and convention hotels. Equally important is to contact the executive in charge of convention planning of corporations/organizations that are scheduled to hold gatherings in your city.

For subjects such as tour transportation, fees, licensing, and additional promotion measures, the same recommendations apply as outlined in Chapter 28.

30

Class Reunions Are Booming: Lots of Business for Reunion Planners

It happens all the time and everywhere. Those who set the idea of a class reunion into motion conveniently disappear until the happy occasion takes place. So busy people get stuck serving on the reunion committee—and they are not happy about it!

The truth is, most everyone relishes such a joyful gathering, but the fact that it takes extensive work to plan a reunion discourages many from volunteering their services. Turning over the total work load to an independent, outside service is now being welcomed by more and more committee members. The demand for professional reunion planning is on the rise. So new is this home-based mini-business, that it is still unknown in some parts of the country.

This means opportunities for people who thrive on organizational detail work. Are you one of them? Do you have plenty of time on hand at this stage in your life? Can you persuade either your energetic spouse or a qualified friend to join you in this endeavor? An efficient team, consisting of two or three individuals, is essential to produce results.

Results mean gaining a substantial market share of the reunion planning business in your community and beyond. And with it go valuable word-of-mouth referrals.

The work of a professional reunion planning service is diverse, time-oriented, yet by no means monotonous. It requires not only patience but also resourcefulness to track down former classmates after as many as thirty-five, forty-five, and even fifty years. Besides locating and inviting these former classmates, you must work out all details for the reunion event. Such arrangements include setting up meeting places, overnight accommodations, eating facilities, activities, possible transportation, entertainment bookings, and photographer. Then there will be additional requests from the committee. And don't count out unexpected problems. They must be dealt with promptly and effectively.

This unique service provides an excellent opportunity to meet a variety of interesting people. Simplify routines and, as a result, enjoy the planning work by delegating tasks to your partner(s) in accordance with their qualifications. A distinct advantage of this ser-

vice is the low start-up investment, though the profit
share going to each partner may grow slowly for the
first few years.

Because this type of service is still unknown in certain regions, flexibility is needed in establishing the fee
schedule. The service team's remuneration is based on a
percentage of the total reunion expenditure. Consequently, accurate monitoring of the latter is essential.

Fond of Reunions?

They are mothers, they are friends, and as a
team of two they are operating the successful Reunion Planning, Inc. Six years ago, Billie Ferguson, who also teaches school
part-time, and her friend Ginny Knoll formed
a home-based service coordinating high
school reunions in their community. After
three reunion assignments the first year, the
gradual service buildup was in step with
their goals and their family obligations. Today, the team's professionally run, computer-operated, home-based business handles
close to twenty high school reunion events
per year. At the height of the season, they
are aided by a number of part-time employees to ensure smooth running of all reunion
arrangements. Although they assert that
they really never get away from the business, the two affable and resourceful women
seem devoted to furthering their flourishing
enterprise.

Your promotional efforts should start with the printing of an attractive folder. Then contact your community's high schools, current class committees, alumni organizations, and local or county-based higher education institutions. And if you happen to live near a military base or installation, by all means include military reunion activities in your reunion planning service. Finally, see the business or city editor of your local newspaper(s). A feature story about your new useful service will spread the word beyond the city's boundaries.

One more important point: hire competent local professionals who can guide you in complying with all community business requirements.

Suggested Reading

Ninkovich, Tom. *Reunion Handbook for School and Military Reunions.* 2d ed. San Francisco: Reunion Research, 1989. (Order from Reunion Research, 3145 Geary Boulevard, #14, San Francisco, CA 94118.)

31

Always in Demand: Telephone Answering at Low Cost

Are you or your spouse housebound and looking for ways to earn an income? Does working as a team appeal to you? If you are people-oriented and enjoy lively daily interaction, here is a fruitful way to capitalize on verbal skills, alertness, and detail-mindedness—even if you are confined to a wheelchair.

Even though sizable professional answering services are well established in most cities, from townships to large metropolitan areas, there is still room for home-based, low-cost answering services. The latter attract a different clientele than the large establishments, namely small business persons and tradespeople. Being away from their workplace for long hours, some owners of small businesses, shops, and offices have tried to solve the problem by installing a telephone answering device. Yet, for a number of reasons, these machines do not always work to the full satisfaction of the business world. The personal answering service can ensure personalized around-the-clock (or morning till evening) call answering, message taking and relaying. Further, clients have access to the service at any time.

How does the service connect with the customer's telephone? The client need only utilize the telephone's "call forwarding" feature. Any client with "call forwarding" has the choice of obtaining this feature from the local telephone company for a modest monthly charge, or listing the answering service number in his or her advertisements.

If you decide to establish such a service, you will find prospective clients among the following businesses: small combination retail/repair services, yard maintenance services, painters, wallpaper hangers, carpet layers, carpenters, as well as the many small construction and renovation contractors. Other prospects are professionals in the decorating trade, real estate salespersons, manufacturers' representatives, and church offices. The last named, in particular, prefer the human voice to mechanical devices for lunchtime, evening, and weekend telephone answering. Furthermore, people who frequently sell used merchandise through newspaper ads or sales bulletins will be worthwhile prospects. While working outside their homes during daytime hours, they are generally concerned about missing calls of genuine prospective buyers. To use your service telephone number in their sales ads would give them the added advantage of call screening—a point worth emphasizing in your own promotion.

Your modest investment—a commercial telephone installation, the usual recordkeeping supplies, and printed promotional materials—plus your low overhead expenses will enable you to offer rates lower than those of larger service companies with personnel and high-tech equipment.

Investigate your community's current monthly and weekly answering service contractual charges and conditions before setting up your own rate schedule and contracts. In many areas the existing monthly rates average $55 for one hundred calls per month.

Your promotion can be launched with weekly classified ads in daily and weekly area newspapers. Emphasize the convenience of around-the-clock personalized answering service for business, trade, and private selling. Stress the advantages of savings and nonrestricted access to your service line.

Subsequently, have colored flyers printed and distribute them to neighborhood business as listed above. Also post circulars or business cards on bulletin boards at food markets and drop them off at building supply centers, lumber dealers, and church offices. Bring the distribution to the attention of the managers of these businesses through follow-up phone calls.

Finally, familiarize yourself with your local zoning ordinance, as well as licensing and tax laws that apply to home-based service businesses. An accountant specializing in small business clients can tailor an accounting system to your service needs.

32

Fond of Children? Plenty of Service Choices

Was your home once filled with laughter and happy children's voices? And now you delight in your lively, bubbly grandchildren when they come to visit you? It's only natural, then, that the care of children entered your mind when you recently contemplated supplementing your present income. But what types of opportunities exist for individuals or couples—at all age levels—in the child-care field?

Several diverse part-time, team-oriented service choices, which mature persons in particular have pursued with success, are weekend-sitting service, afterschool care for schoolchildren, children's escort service, and children's party planning. What are the major requirements and rewards? No matter which of these activities is undertaken, the service owner must have a good character, demonstrating responsibility and a commitment to serve children and their parents well. Physical fitness is also indispensable. Any devotion to child care is bound to be rewarded with enjoyment and satisfaction in daily care activities. A fact of life in this field is that there will be times when profitable earnings take a back seat to the personal rewards gained from working with the very young.

Let's first look at the *weekend-sitting service*. A genuine need for weekend child-sitters in the family home will be steadily on the rise, as long as resort hotels and airlines continue to offer an increasing number of attractive weekend and minivacation packages for couples and individuals. Other weekend-sitting needs may arise from family emergencies, or when the parent or parents simply need a short break from child care. Most of the time, these parents rule out the family's regular school-age baby-sitter for the weekend-sitting job. They tend to look for a responsible adult, or adult couple, who has demonstrated good rapport with children and comes highly recommended.

The weekend service begins with your moving into the client's home on Friday afternoon, when you receive your specific instructions from the parents. After their departure, you immediately take on the responsibility of caring for the children. You will supervise their activities, feed them, perhaps make plans to take them out on Saturday or Sunday afternoon. The assignment generally ends Sunday evening, or whenever the parents return.

Compensation for such weekend-sitting service can very well average $100 for the couple, plus the food and lodging for the service period. Depending on the length of the assignment, and its demand within the community, the rates can easily exceed this amount.

Another popular service is *afterschool care for children*, usually between the ages of six and fourteen. The public is very much aware of the fact that working parents do not relish the idea of leaving their school-age children unsupervised and alone at home, often for hours.

This kind of service is frequently pursued by former educators. Educational experience and innovative organizational methods are the proven ingredients of a thriving afterschool service. In addition, the availability of ample space (one or two comfortable rooms) is mandatory. Preferably, the designated area should be equipped with several work-tables, comfortable seating, and a few student desks. Aside from the supervision of the children's homework, recreational activities and snacks must be provided. According to newspaper reports, some service owners have taught their charges to play chess, and other stimulating games, with impressive results.

Equally promising for a married couple or other twosome is the more seasonal *children's escort service*. There is no limit to imaginative excursion planning. For example, children can be taken to the zoo, science museum, or theme park; on picnics, hikes, or trips to the roller rink. Other popular attractions are children's theater, concert, circus, puppet show, sports event, even mystery tour.

A vital factor in this particular service business is the availability of adequate and safe transportation. Depending on the number of participating children, vehicle and driver may have to be chartered, and additional adults hired to supervise the children. These extra expenses will naturally affect the per-child fee. The undertaking can still net fair profit for the service owner.

Another useful and sought-after service in certain regions is *children's party planning*. Today, more than ever before, birthday parties for children of various ages have become lavish and imaginative. The planning includes food-catering arrangements, and everything from invitations and decorations to entertainment and prizes. Originality in party planning will ensure referrals from satisfied customers.

If you decide to involve yourself with any one of these services, be certain to strive for excellence. It will earn you recognition and referrals. Your reputation depends on it.

All types of child care are regulated by states and municipalities. Familiarize yourself with the existing state license laws, local fire, zoning, and tax regulations, as well as bonding and insurance requirements.

Reputable local professionals (attorney, accountant, and insurance professional) should aid you in complying with all business requirements. Also establish some references.

Your low-cost promotional efforts can start with the printing of an attractive flyer for distribution in local neighborhoods. Hand out copies at elementary and junior high schools, and at homes and apartments. Post flyers on bulletin boards of libraries, women's clubs, civic organizations, and churches. This can take your service business off to a quick start. From there on, you can depend primarily on referrals.

Suggested Reading

Benton, Barbara. *The Baby Sitter's Handbook.* New York: Morrow, 1981.

Larsky, Vicki. *Dear Babysitter Handbook.* Deephaven, Minn.: Book Peddlers, 1990.

Manning, Barbralu. *Kids Mean Business: How to Turn Your Love of Children into a Profitable and Wonderfully Satisfying Business.* Boulder, Colo.: Live Oak, 1985.

33

Animal Lovers: Here Comes the Pet Express

So you are an animal lover. Probably, at one time or another, you have surrounded yourself with lovable kittens, playful puppies, a chirping canary, or even an assortment of hamsters, rabbits, clucking hens, and quacking ducks.

Would you consider venturing into a nonconventional pet-care service field? No, it's not sitting, boarding, grooming, or training—it's pet-taxiing. It's new and ever so challenging! (Those who find pet-sitting more appealing can turn to the service profile in Chapter 12.)

Pet transportation may be just what you are looking for. Vital to this service is a suitable vehicle. Do you own a van or station-wagon? If so, compartmentalize a section of the vehicle to accommodate the transport of house pets. You'll also need to purchase a number of pet carriers, available in a variety of affordable models at wholesale sources. To increase your chances for success, engage your pet-loving spouse or a friend as an equal partner in the new venture. Both of you will find it to be a stimulating undertaking, involving daily exciting encounters with more than one pet.

Is there really a demand for a pet carrier in the community? Of course there is. For example, who takes

Rover, the house pet of a working couple, to his regular veterinary checkups or grooming appointments? And what about the excitable French poodle Gigi, whose stomach ailments need veterinary attention? Her owner, a frail elderly woman, still drives a rather spacious vintage car, but is she able to handle both the car and high-strung Gigi at the same time? And who drives the terminally ill terrier Muffin to the veterinary euthanasia service, or to the local pet cemetery to lighten the burden of the pet's heavy-hearted owner? For all these diverse needs, the new pet carrier service can come to the rescue of working and elderly pet owners alike.

Begin by researching the local market potential. Contact your area's veterinary hospitals and make the rounds of local pet-grooming establishments. Get a feeling for your community's pet-care market and determine whether it can support a carrier service. You may have to generate additional business in neighboring communities.

Also look into the local zoning, licensing, and tax laws, including bonding and liability coverage. Reputable local professionals, such as an attorney, accountant, and insurance professional, can counsel you on all business requirements.

In the Midwest some new pet carrier services have become quite successful. Transportation fees start at $10, plus the cost of any supplies. They can go as high as $75 and $100, depending on the distance covered and individualized services rendered. Judging from the experiences of those in the pet-care trade, pet owners are willing to pay a reasonable fee if they are convinced their pet will receive the best possible care.

Media advertising will help you reach a maximum

audience. In the beginning, classified and even small display ads in your local daily newspaper(s) and weekly suburban papers will give you the exposure you need. And a listing in the Yellow Pages will spread the word about your service throughout the year.

If your service is the first of its type in the community, business or city editors of your newspaper(s) might be willing to give you some valuable publicity by carrying a feature story about the new service.

© Polly Keener '91

Furthermore, have business cards and flyers printed and distribute them to veterinary hospitals, pet shops, all establishments catering to pet care and supplies, as well as area kennel clubs, canine training centers, dog and cat breeders, and pet cemeteries. Also post your flyers on bulletin boards of upscale apartment buildings, senior citizens' communities, and civic organizations.

Emphasize in all your advertising material that you

will only handle house pets. This will rule out unexpected requests for taxiing nasty reptiles or unruly lion cubs.

Suggested Reading

Alderton, David. *The Dog Care Manual.* New York: Barrons, 1986.

Nicholas, Barbara. *The Portable Pet.* Harvard, Mass.: Harvard Common Press, 1983.

34

Rental Services: From Maids to Bicycles

Fifteen years ago, who had ever heard of renting a maid, a cook, a plant, a bicycle? The rent-anything phenomenon of the eighties is now being taken for granted. And there is no softening of this market in sight.

Yet not everyone is willing to run a rental service. Many of these rental businesses are not risk free and are often slow to catch on. The service owner must demonstrate entrepreneurial spirit, alertness, perseverance, and a grasp of business fundamentals. But for a qualified, experienced individual, or team of mature persons, this field offers stimulating activities and promising income possibilities.

Let's start by examining *Rent-a-Maid* agencies, which are doing well in some larger cities. These agencies coexist with commercial cleaning services, but unlike the latter, they furnish the maid's labor only for a specified list of services and have the client provide all job supplies. The service matches the client's needs with a maid trained in the service area requested. The work can range from all-day home cleaning, to errands plus some cleaning, to fixing simple meals and cleaning up afterward. For dinner-party preparations, serving, and cleanup, clients occasionally request two maids. Working hours for assistants at dinner parties generally start in the afternoon and run through late evening hours. Rented serving maids furnish their own uniforms.

Success in this business depends largely on maintaining an up-to-date registry of dependable, experienced persons. Such part-time opportunities appeal to many applicants. The quality of the personnel pool is vital to a thriving business. For personnel recruitment, the service owner must primarily rely on advertisements.

The client pays the service fee directly to the service owner, who, in turn, compensates the self-employed recruits. Generally, a minimum of 20 percent of the total client charge is the remuneration for the owner.

Well suited for larger communities is the *Rent-a-Cook* service. Again, the availability of qualified and reliable professionals, such as chefs, cooks, and food-service assistants, as well as bartenders, is paramount.

Business can be generated from local hosts and hostesses, civic clubs and other organizations, and churches. Churches, in particular, can be considered good prospects because many maintain a well-equipped kitchen on their property yet lack qualified personnel to fulfill their occasional gastronomical needs. Besides, churches and other organizations and institutions frequently rent their social hall, including kitchen facilities, to the public. It is often a source of income for them to take advantage of the brisk demand for reception and other social function facilities.

It will also be helpful for the owner of a rent-a-cook service to be knowledgeable in the field of gastronomy. On many occasions, he or she must function in an advisory capacity and be a judge of the recruited professionals. As with other rent-a-professional services, compensation for the owner generally amounts to a minimum of 20 percent of the total client charge.

Although the rent-a-cook service is limited to furnishing the labor only, if so desired, it can be expanded in stages into a party-supply business.

The proliferating rental services have penetrated other business areas as well. The most notable area is the trendy *merchandise field.* Everyone is familiar with truck, tool, tuxedo, and costume rentals. Some of them have speedily developed into the "big-name boys" of this booming service field, and they now eagerly franchise their services. Yet numerous smaller versions can be expediently managed by a business-oriented individual or a team of two. Close attention must be paid to the availability of adequate display and storage space, existing zoning laws, and merchandise investment. Other essential prerequisites are some purchasing skills and connections to quality merchandise wholesalers.

Some proven money-makers in the merchandise rental business are various types of fitness equipment, ranging from treadmills, climbers, and weight-lifting equipment to bicycles, golf clubs, and winter sport supplies. Other flourishing small rental services specialize in wallpaper removal equipment, wedding attire, and plants. (Plant rental is profiled in Chapter 26.) Now that the consumer's appetite has been whetted, the sky is the limit as far as new rental ideas are concerned.

Comply with your state's and community's regulations covering rental agencies by investigating the zoning, licensing, and tax laws. A certified public accountant specializing in small-business clients can furnish an appropriate accounting system, while an attorney and an insurance professional can counsel you on the start-up requirements.

35

A Flair for Fashion and Modeling? Some Stylish Opportunities

Have you ever walked down the runway in a fashion show, poised and coolheaded while hundreds of gazing eyes were centered on both you and the garment you were modeling? You did? Then you should be congratulated. If you don't have modeling experience, perhaps you've been a fashion consultant, or a buyer in a large department or specialty store.

A sales background, good public relations, and the

ability to communicate style and color to others are a winning combination. Regardless of your age, these qualifications will help you succeed in any of several fashion- or modeling-related ventures. Having a support person on your side, either spouse or friend who complements your talents, will enhance your prospects for success.

The pursuit of fashion-related services appears to be enjoyable and profitable. At least that is the impression one gets when speaking to enterprising women operating their own fashion business. They all look stunning, appear self-assured, and seem prosperous.

Are you ready to set up an in-home fashion consumer service? Give the business an attractive name, pack the seasonal fashion and accessory collection into your car, and become a *mobile wardrobe and image consultant*. This is an activity you can pursue on either a part- or full-time basis. The first step is to contact the national office of the direct-sales fashion and cosmetics company of your choice. A cross-section of direct-sales companies is featured in Appendix A. By all means, check out the chosen company and, preferably, contact and interview current company representatives before making any commitment. Depending on the corporation's policy, you may have to travel to its headquarters to take a several-day training course. After graduating to certified consultant status, and according to your efforts, you can under certain circumstances rapidly move up the organizational ladder.

Once you decide to invest in a distributor kit, the corporation generally furnishes ample fashion literature, samples, and a complete set of forms for sales transactions. The investment amount varies markedly from company to company, ranging from a minimum of $75 to several hundred dollars.

The Stylish Image Consultant

Interested in improving the image or self-esteem of women clients? A genuine winner in this field is Donna Murray, a personable career woman. For six years affiliated with a nationally known direct-sales company as an independent image consultant, the tall, self-assured Donna rose through dedicated work to the rank of regional executive director within the company's sales organization. Together with her sales team of over 150 recruited independent consultants in various larger cities, she offers color analysis, fashionable clothing, skin care, and cosmetics mainly to career women in their homes. The company's multilevel marketing plan assures those in executive positions, as well as the multiplying sales force, of scaled profit sharing. In her lucrative executive position, Donna appears extremely pleased to share in the experience of changing the image and lives of loyal customers—and values the rapid broadening of her recruits' sales base. This consultation/sales work offers splendid opportunities for women dissatisfied in other sales fields, the image consultant contends.

If fashion network marketing appeals to you, turn to the Chapter 52 profile, "Popular Direct Sales/Network Marketing." It presents a detailed account of advantages and disadvantages you may encounter in the multilevel marketing field.

Perhaps you wish to take another route. Remain an *independent fashion consultant* and explore wholesale sources of designer fashions on your own. You can later expand the service to costume jewelry, lingerie, and cosmetics. If you don't want to handle cosmetics yourself, you may want to contract with a makeup studio for your clients' cosmetic make-overs. Note that your independence status will require a larger investment of time and money, and considerable business know-how. The designer fashion approach makes it necessary to target a distinct upscale clientele. Depending on your position within the community, such a route may require special efforts, perhaps the marketing strategy of a dedicated teammate.

Regardless of what direction you take, you will have to build up a loyal following, preferably centering on the career woman. You will cater to her individual needs, with particular emphasis on saving time and matching clothing to her personality or life-style.

Does the fashion field appear to be crowded in your area? You have the option of directing your marketing efforts toward the mature career woman. Women's professional organizations and women's club meetings are valuable sources for prospective clients. And don't hesitate to contact large local corporations, financial institutions, and other sizable employers. They might just be willing to arrange for group program presentations or style consultations.

Setting up a financially rewarding *home-based modeling agency* is another choice available to you, although it's a competitive field. Knowledge of the modeling business and managerial skill are essential. A capable teammate will prove helpful.

As a modeling agent, you may want to recruit female and male models in your own age bracket. Or, whatever your age, consider concentrating on the lucrative over-fifty age group. The business community has long recognized the importance of this steadily growing population segment with its imposing purchasing power. Notice, for example, advertising agencies now make increasing use of mature models.

Aside from the substantial business generated by advertising agencies, others engaging models of all age groups are department stores, clothing stores, boutiques, photographers, beauty salons, manufacturers needing product demonstrators at trade shows, and conventions and exhibition centers.

The owner of the modeling agency receives a percentage of the total model fee paid by the client. Investigate your local and neighboring city markets for recruiting conditions and agency regulations, as well as for guidance in establishing your own fee schedule.

Study the latest books on the fashion business available in your local public library. Also examine your area's zoning, licensing, and tax laws. And finally, contact a certified public accountant, who can devise a suitable accounting system for your new service business, and a competent attorney and insurance professional, who can assist you in complying with your community's small business requirements.

Suggested Reading

Lant, Jeffrey L. *The Consultant's Kit.* 2d ed. Cambridge, Mass.: JLA Publications, 1981.

36

Home-based Cooking Classes: Income in Your Kitchen

Wouldn't you love to augment your present income and have fun at the same time? Are you a trained chef, institutional cook, food editor, or home economics teacher, perhaps missing the work you once thoroughly enjoyed? Or have you over the years earned the reputation of being an admirable family cook who surprises family and friends with memorable culinary delights?

Let's look closely at the workings of a home-based cooking school. An important prerequisite for such a school is the availability of a sizable, fully-equipped, attractive kitchen. You may have one in your own home. If not, you have the option of leasing a first-rate facility at a central location. Some clubs, organizations, and churches lease their kitchens on a regular basis. In such instances, your investment would be limited to the purchase of necessary kitchen equipment and utensils. A helper for cleanup is needed under all circumstances. This teammate—either your spouse, or a friend, or a family member—can also stand by as demonstration assistant, as well as food buyer, and can taxi your haulable equipment to and from cooking destinations outside your home. Also engage a team of competent professionals (attorney, accountant, insurance professional) to counsel you on compliance with your community's specific business regulations.

Cooking-class themes can be as diverse as your imagination, your skills, and your locale permit. You can stretch your teaching from quick cuisine, healthy cooking for two, and diet meals to party feasts, ethnic specialties, and cooking classes for children. Or give instructions in baking breads, preparing specialty desserts, assembling exquisite hors d'oeuvres, or creating summer party fare.

The profit margin built into the tuition fee for a cooking class depends largely on the demand for such service in a given geographic area. Study carefully the market in your own town or city, and in neighboring communities. Expenses will vary and are determined by the cost of the basics: rent, utilities, hired labor, individualized foodstuff, and supplies.

Whereas some cooking classes may warrant only a onetime, several-hours meeting (afternoon, evening, or Saturday morning), other once-a-week gatherings can be spread over a three- to four-week period.

At least in the beginning, you may have to rely primarily on personal contacts to generate interest in your cooking classes. In addition to placing your business cards and printed class announcements on bulletin boards of food markets, approach the managers of wine and beverage stores, and of houseware outlets. Likewise, contact owners of specialty and gourmet food stores and suggest some weekend sampling (specially prepared cooking-class samples) for the benefit of their customers. Any proprietor will gladly surround your sampling table with complementary merchandise and beverages. At the same time, publicize your class schedule. (Always set a registration deadline.) Finally, volunteer your cooking talent for short demonstrations or lectures at club meetings and other social gatherings. And place small but effective display ads with class schedules in the life-style section of your local papers' weekend editions.

Turn to Chapter 27, "Gourmet Chefs and Other Cooks—Taste These Possibilities," for a variety of other activities in the food service field.

Suggested Reading

Shown, Janet. *Freelance Foodcrafting*. Boulder, Colo.: Live Oak, 1983.

37

||||➤ ◄||||

For Sewing Experts, Opportunities with or Without Needle and Thread

If you have sewing skills and some professional experience in the field, you can choose between several profitable traditional sewing services. But what if you have developed an appreciation for a garment's style, color, texture, and workmanship yet lack the ability to sew professionally? Don't despair! In this chapter you will be given the opportunity to examine a new, stimulating money-making venture where professional sewing is *not* a prerequisite.

Everyone is familiar with the most common sewing service: the *independent seamstress or dressmaker*. Nowadays, it is not difficult to acquire a loyal clientele if the dressmaker turns out well-fitting clothing combined with good workmanship. Most dressmakers set up a sewing workroom in their home. Customer satisfaction will ensure not only a tidy profit but also rapid word-of-mouth recommendations.

With or without a partner, you can establish a slightly different version of a sewing business. Rent office space in a shopping center or in a supermarket complex. It can easily be turned into a dressmaker studio. Thus you can charge prime fees for studio-made quality garments.

Increase your profit by carrying popular fabrics and linings for resale.

Here are other sewing service variations: Specialize in alterations or cater to people in need of customized clothing. Concentrate on suit tailoring, bridal wear, party dresses, or costumes (for costume events, ballet schools, school plays). Or consider the fields of customized quilting, bedspreads, slipcovers, or draperies and window shades.

If you enjoy teaching others, a *sewing school* can become a satisfying money-maker. Taking sewing classes will be desired by homemakers for years to come. If your home-based workplace is not suitable for sewing demonstrations, rent office space in a shopping center, mall, or supermarket complex, or contract with a sewing machine retailer.

Plan classes with distinct consumer appeal. Besides dressmaking, other popular subjects are blazer and pant tailoring, working with knits, the making of children's clothing, lingerie, costumes (plan just ahead of the season), and alterations. It is imperative to have attractively finished samples on hand or displayed at your class facility.

What if any of these services suffer from the slow-start syndrome? Well, why not simultaneously offer to the public a *consultation service*? Many consumers embark on ambitious sewing projects but soon run into difficulties. At this point, they are looking desperately for professional help and don't know where to turn. Such a consultation service will take very little of your time yet will bring in welcome revenues. Be certain to emphasize this service in all your promotional material and to spread the word through local fabric stores.

And here is the opportunity for those without sewing expertise—it's the little-known sewing registry, or *sewing referral service*. It is well suited for residents of medium- and large-size communities. Good business sense and some managerial skills will be useful, and teaming up with a mate or friend who complements your talents will enhance your chances for success.

In this "bring-two-parties together" business, the sewing service pays you a commission, or finder's fee (minimum 10 percent), on each completed work transaction. Or consider a semiannual registration fee for all sewing services or firms that sign up with your registry.

How does it work? A consumer in need of a certain type of sewing service calls the number of your referral service. At that time, you will furnish a minimum of two names of registered service owners or firms in the requested category.

There are plenty of specialized sewing services to approach for a referral sign-up. They include designer dressmaking, general dressmaking, women's and men's tailoring, party dressing, bridal wear, alterations, children's clothing. Other categories in demand are mending, accessorizing, making customized slipcovers, draperies and window shades, quilted bedspreads. You can also expect the public to inquire about specialty products, such as dressing dolls, T-shirt and apron making, novelties. Additionally, you will receive requests for needle-work specialties, such as smocking, quilting, monogramming, and designer knitwear.

The recruitment of reputable, trustworthy sewing services, several from each category, is an investment in time. Investigate the proprietors or firms before you ask them to sign up. Be sure to check them out with the local Better Business Bureau and examine their finished products. Later, when asking them to join your service, stress the fact that this association will stimulate their business, especially during off-season slowdowns.

Limited financial investment is one of the venture's advantages. You may need to install a separate telephone and invest in reliable answering equipment and office supplies. It will be useful to have an accounting service set up an effective bookkeeping system. The cost of the promotional campaign, plus materials, should be modest.

Furthermore, you may find a spinoff activity of the above attractive and worth exploring—become an *agent for small sewing firms* by selling their finished products. The lines may include infant wear, evening bags, or novelty items. Accept only marketable merchandise and collect a commission on each negotiated bulk sale. Merchandise lots can be sold to specialty stores, boutiques, gift shops, department stores. You can also service bazaars, fairs, and other fund-raising events held by various organizations in your area.

Promotional activities for sewing school and referral service can start with the printing of business cards and an attractive flyer. Distribute them to fabric shops, interior decorators, beauty salons, food markets, laundromats, schools, women's and fitness clubs, apartment buildings, residential neighborhoods, and Welcome Wagon organizations. A Yellow Page listing will spread the message to neighboring communities.

Examine your local zoning ordinance and license and tax regulations. Competent local professionals can assist you in complying with all requirements. And if your sewing talents need updating and fine-tuning, choose from a variety of excellent and informative books available at your public library. They cover topics ranging from pattern making to needlework specialties.

Suggested Reading

Brabec, Barbara. *Creative Cash*. 4th ed. Huntington Beach, Calif.: Aames-Allen, 1986. (Order from BF Books, 941 Populus Place, Sunnyvale, CA 94086.)

Smith, Judith, and Allan Smith. *Sewing for Profits*. Lake Park, Fla.: Success Advertising and Publishing, 1984.

38

Secretarial and Word-processing Services

Seasoned administrative assistants, secretaries, or super clerks, your chances have never been better to rid yourself of a boss, demonstrate your capabilities, and turn your experience into hard cash! With pride, competence, and enthusiasm, entrepreneurs have carried the secretarial service business to amazing success. Wouldn't you like to invest your time and talents to become an independent and respected service owner? Demand for a variety of stenographic and word processing exists in most urban areas. Let's focus on the most common types.

Are you highly skilled in taking dictation and furnishing quality tape transcriptions but prefer to limit working hours to certain times and days? Then setting up a free-lance *stenographic and transcription service* would be an ideal way to supplement your income. Since such services are frequently needed on short notice, or on an emergency basis, as well as after office hours, the compensation will exceed average rates. In time, it will add up to a tidy annual sum for your part-time work.

Good stationery typing and transcription equipment, a suitable workplace in your home, and reliable transportation represent only a minimal investment. Then you are ready to give express service to traveling executives, visiting lecturers, speakers, public relations offices, and local small businesses.

Depending on the size of your community, your promotional efforts should be directed toward hotels, public relations firms, convention centers, speaker agencies, and transportation terminals. Other prospective clients for your new service are local corporate headquarters, travel agencies, lecturing facilities, and larger educational institutions.

Another type of business you might consider is the *secretarial* or *word-processing service*. In many areas, it has remarkable growth potential. The service can be launched on a part-time, one-person basis, or with a congenial partner. Starting small—with a low-overhead, easily manageable business—will enable you to readily test your community's demand for your service. If warranted, you can expand it to a business with ten or more employees, and, of course, any size in between.

Obviously, communities with a healthy business climate need a variety of secretarial services. It is essential to first take a close look at your own work preferences, as well as the existing competition, before setting up your service.

To get a foothold on the local market, it would be wise for a new service to concentrate on only one of the multiple business sectors. For example, if you have previously worked in the medical and health-care field, your preference would be taking on transcription work from physicians or overflow work from health-care offices, hospitals, and similar institutions. As a former legal secretary, you can service attorneys, legal organizations, title companies. Then there is the academic community. You may want to specialize in typing term papers, theses, manuscripts, lecture scripts, résumés, reports, research papers. In the fields of finance and accounting, you can obtain overflow work from various accounting firms. If you have formerly worked for a manufacturing company, or in the small business community, you may feel confident about adding clerical work to your service. You can offer to do invoicing and bulk mailings, in addition to typing letters, business reports, customer listings, labels. You can even offer to handle holiday-card signing and addressing.

If you don't have enough workspace in your home, rent a small office or store space in a central location close to office complexes. You need adequate office supplies, an electronic office typewriter, some basic office machines. You can purchase used equipment or rent machines with options to buy. This should get you through the start-up months. Soon afterward, invest your profits in a word processor.

To establish your fee schedule, determine the going rates in your own and neighboring communities. Modify them to fit your needs. Then consult a team of competent local professionals (attorney, accountant, insurance professional) to advise you on your area's service business requirements.

An attractive business card together with a perfectly executed letter and rate schedule will be needed to introduce your service to the kind of businesses and professionals you want to serve. After a couple of weeks, make the rounds and follow up with personal phone calls. Also, place some classified ads in the press that caters to the local business world. A listing in the Yellow Pages will be beneficial as well.

Suggesting Reading

Murray, Jean Wilson. *Starting and Operating a Word Processing Service.* Babylon, N.Y.: Pilot Books, 1983. (Order from Pilot Books, 103 Cooper Street, Babylon, N.Y. 11702.)

Temple, Mary. *How to Start a Secretarial and Business Service.* Babylon, N.Y.: Pilot Books, 1978. (Order from Pilot Books.)

39

Become a Small Manufacturer: Anything Goes, from Sweaters to Jams

Still occasionally dreaming about your brainstorm for a new product? Have you finalized your pet project, the building of the perfect hostess cart, which showed early promise of consumer appeal? Or perhaps you concocted a divine-tasting cold-cut dressing. Whatever the product idea—and if only for a split second—you may have visualized the product's conquest of the world markets. What an indescribable feeling! Well, if you have a *practical* idea, it's never too late to do something about turning it into a desirable product and start selling it in your own hometown.

Most likely, you are one of those inventive and resourceful individuals who can readily hand- or machine-produce a useful, marketable product. Perhaps family members or friends have been urging you for some time to capitalize on your ingenuity. The product you have been concentrating on may be a family food favorite—a special bread, sauce, jam, or cake. It could be an article of a totally different nature. As a master carpenter, or as a mechanic or mechanically inclined person, you have developed a versatile home tool or a practical or decorative product. And if you are a craftsperson, you may turn out one-of-a-kind jewelry, leather accessories, handwoven rugs/wallhangings, or even fashionable hand-knitted sweaters.

With due respect to your family's and friends' enthusiasm, a venture to market your own product must begin with honest self-analysis. Determine whether you have the stamina to work long hours, if necessary, to satisfy future demand. When it comes to marketing, do you have the confidence to go out and offer the product to retail establishments? Other important areas that must be researched: possible investment in costly new or used equipment, availability of adequate workspace, and product packaging and labeling. Consideration must also be given to existing food-preparation or product-safety laws, as well as zoning and licensing regulations in your area. Whatever type of service you choose, a competent local team of professionals should be hired to aid you in complying with local business requirements, and in establishing your business procedures.

Unusual food products should first be test-marketed at food markets. Offer free samples and sell the product in small-quantity packages as an introductory offer; include a simple, informative flyer with all merchandise. The public's reaction should be closely studied. Clubs, church bazaars, local fairs, and farmers' markets present additional consumer test opportunities. If the results are encouraging, possibly after some product modifications, the food product can then be offered to convenience stores, snack and sandwich shops, luncheonettes, as well as country eateries and inns.

Craft articles made of wood, metal, textiles, or other materials can be put to the test with the cooperation of supermarkets and specialty stores that carry unusual merchandise. If the public response is satisfactory, finalize the product's pricing and negotiate with store owners to sell the item through their sales outlets.

Another option is to rent space at shopping malls, fairs, and other special event sites. Craftspersons have the additional choice of engaging a craft broker. Brokers and agents are always looking for interesting new objects to promote and to sell. Although these options will curtail the profit, in the long run they can save you time and headaches, and even increase the sales volume.

It requires patience and perseverance to successfully market hand-made, homemade, or small-production-line items. Expect a slow start-up period, but with effective market tryouts and persistence, your efforts will gradually lead to a steadily growing income.

Suggested Reading

Long, Steve, and Cindy Long. *You Can Make Money from Your Arts and Crafts.* Scotts Valley, Calif.: Mark Publications, 1988.

Null, Gary, and R. Simonson. *How to Turn Your Ideas into Dollars.* Babylon, N.Y.: Pilot Books, 1978. (Order from Pilot Books, 103 Cooper Street, Babylon, NY 11702.)

Small Business Administration. *Ideas into Dollars.* (See Appendix B for details on how to order this and other useful SBA pamphlets.)

Part IV

Home-based Businesses for People with a Business Background

40

||➤ ⬅||

Good Sales Ability? Use It to Buy and to Sell

Last week you heard your neighbor tell a woeful tale about purchasing a secondhand freezer, and just yesterday a friend told you that she couldn't sell her old stove when she moved to a new home. Both times, weren't you thinking, isn't there a smoother and more effective way for local sellers and buyers to interact?

No doubt, you have seen those weekly or bimonthly publications devoted to used merchandise trading. Yet there are other ways of selling and buying merchandise, which venturesome men and women have turned into gratifying and lucrative businesses. One of them is a home-operated buying and selling service. Any well-organized, efficient person with sales background and an affinity for sales work can set up such a business.

You may want to start out on a part-time basis. Once you enjoy seeing your service grow, turn it into a full-fledged venture. Along the way, consider taking a teammate or partner aboard.

Frankly, the start-up period will require alertness and some uphill work efforts. But then, most sales people enjoy a challenge. Your first step is to observe closely the buying and selling habits of consumers by surveying relevant local advertisements and bazaars and other events at which used merchandise is sold. In the beginning, it's wise to limit the variety of traded merchandise. Don't try to be all things to all people right from the start! Concentrate first on trading within a specific used-merchandise sector, such as electrical appliances, furniture, patio, or other household furnishings. Once you have established yourself among local buyers and sellers, you can easily expand the merchandise field.

A 5 percent after-sale service commission on all items is widely accepted. You may be able to secure a higher commission on scarce merchandise.

Effective, not necessarily expensive, local newspaper advertisements will be essential to draw buyers' attention to your service. At the early stage, contact the majority of sellers of used merchandise through their classified newspaper ads and bulletin board notices. Have a flyer printed to reach the selling and buying consumer groups. Then have copies posted at food markets, laundromats, clubs, churches, apartment and office complexes. In-house publications of large local employers are an effective medium to spread the word of your service. Finally, look into the reasonable spot-advertising rates of local radio stations, and buy time on the station that reaches the type of audience you are interested in. The station with the lowest rates may not be aimed at listeners you want to target.

Besides promotional costs, a reliable telephone answering machine is one of the few necessary investments. (Set up a file with the name and phone number of all inquirers. Include even those whose needs go beyond your current trading range because one day, when you expand your business, they may become prospective clients.)

Also invest in the services of a reputable attorney, certified public accountant, insurance professional, and banker. They can steer you through your area's existing service-related ordinances and business laws, and the accountant in particular will be in a position to set up an applicable bookkeeping system for your service.

Suggested Reading

Girard, Joe. *How to Sell Anything to Anybody.* New York: Warner, 1979.

Johnson, Spencer, M.D., and Larry Wilson. *The One Minute Sales Person.* New York: Avon Books, 1984.

41

Antique Expert: Become a Rep or Agent

Are you fascinated by charming Victorian furniture pieces and quaint accessories? Perhaps you genuinely enjoy looking at and examining nineteenth-century European porcelain figurines or fanciful Tiffany glass shades and vases. If you consider yourself knowledgeable of the antique trade, note what others with professional experience have done and examine available choices for gratifying part- or full-time business ventures.

First, there is the most popular opportunity: *represent an antique dealer* at area and regional exhibitions and at other special events. A good way to start your planning is to locate a schedule of your region's antique shows and fairs. Then observe the exhibitors when visiting some of the shows. Make personal contact with dealers to determine which ones are interested in having reliable and competent representation at future antique shows. It is no secret that many dealers, especially those engaged in multiple business activities, do not care to travel the exhibition and show circuit. They consider it a loss of valuable time.

Take into account the dealer's reputation and credibility when weighing offers and suggestions. Draw up a simple contract if satisfied with the proposed arrangements. Incorporate in the contract any pricing and list your commission on each item that you will sell at a firm price, or conclude any other satisfactory payment arrangement.

Another business choice is *selling antiques on a consignment basis.* This is how it works. After obtaining consignment lots from one or several dealer sources, the entrepreneur sells the merchandise to the public at shows or special sales events at consignment-plus-percentage price. Necessary business savvy, experience, and accurate inventory and accounting procedure notwithstanding, consignment buying and selling remain quite popular within the antique trade.

The activity of an *antique trade agent* is another service variation suitable for individuals with trade skills and extensive merchandise sources. Yet this type of service will make it necessary to engage knowledgeable independent salespersons who will do the actual selling for you at shows and permanent public display facilities (malls, hotel lobbies, terminals). The calculation of all expenses and the subsequently established pricing of the merchandise require great care. Particularly in the beginning, the pricing may have to be reviewed periodically.

For each of the described services, the availability of reliable and ample transportation is essential. Above all, physical fitness is required in order to transport and handle massive, as well as delicate, merchandise. Frequently, simple display accommodations need to be set up. Hiring outside help to assist you with these displays would add considerably to your selling expenses; if possible, get low-cost assistance from a family member instead. On the other hand, it pays to engage the services of competent local professionals, such as an attorney, accountant, insurance professional, and, most likely, banker. They will counsel you on all aspects of local business requirements.

If necessary, strengthen your knowledge of antiques by attending some classes at your local adult education institution. Also, your public library should carry a number of updated publications on the subject.

Suggested Reading

Kovel, Ralph, and Terry Kovel. *Kovel's Antiques and Collectibles Price List.* 23d ed. New York: Crown, 1990.

————. *Kovel's Know Your Antiques.* Rev. ed. New York: Crown, 1981.

————. *Kovel's Know Your Collectibles*. New York: Crown, 1981.

42

Was Research Work Part of Your Past? Turn It into Profit!

Perhaps, at one time or another, you have worked in a public or institutional library, in a corporation or bank marketing research department, or in a medical research facility. And you enjoyed it! Consider starting a home-based research service. It's lucrative and stimulating work which can be done at hours of your own choosing.

Knowledgeable managers agree that the look-things-up pressure in offices throughout the country cannot be relieved with a flip of the computer switch. Before marketing data can be fed into a computer for final processing, research legwork must be pursued, often on a one-to-one, and time-consuming, basis. In today's competitive climate, even the smallest commercial enterprise depends on a sales-related information flow to keep either production, merchandise, or creative output moving.

Yet many small companies do not have resources to maintain an in-house research department. These companies have streamlined work forces who have no time to compile marketing information or mailing lists. That means more and more manufacturers, wholesalers, retailers, service firms, tradespeople, professional firms, and health-care providers are turning to outside research firms. It's far more economical.

Through made-to-order projects for such businesses and professionals, a small research service can prove its strength and flexibility. Notably, wholesale, trade, and consumer directories and listings are vital marketing sources for the business community.

If you are seriously considering such a service, familiarize yourself with the latest research tools and sources. Start by paying several visits to your main public library. A librarian can direct you to the newest computerized business information sources. Take plenty of notes. Then relax, for you may be overwhelmed by the sheer abundance of source material. At this point, let the data onslaught sink in gradually. Most likely, the exposure to such a wealth of information will eventually trigger ideas for future application of the materials.

Likewise, visit local publishers of directories, newspaper data centers, bank libraries. Make use of any college or university libraries in your area; some of them have extensive national data on file.

And if some of your future clients request international research information, don't panic! An abundance of national and international data is awaiting you in New York at the World Trade Center. You can tap the sizable United Nations data center, the numerous international trade associations, or branch offices of foreign chambers of commerce. You can also communicate with the trade attaché of any major foreign embassy in Washington. Most will be helpful in locating desired pertinent international market data. There's no need to leave town to get information from any of these sources; just make a phone call or send out a fax on your computer.

Some area market testing may be in order before establishing a fee schedule. Also examine research service rates in neighboring cities. Hourly charges are customary, although much depends on the nature of the project and on client demand. Some experience and a thorough expense analysis will put you in a position to finalize your fees. Set fees high enough so you're generously compensated for your work but low enough to stay competitive in the local market. And note that if your business is a success and demand becomes intense, you can easily engage qualified free-lancers to do the tedious legwork.

Your promotional efforts should center on an introductory letter to sales or marketing executives. This mailing should include a printed folder that outlines your services and rates, and which stresses your ability to deliver research/marketing information tailored to the client's needs. A follow-up telephone call or personal visit is essential. You should also spread the word about your service through occasional classified or small display ads in the business section of local newspapers and in business newsletters. Try to persuade the editors of these publications to print a write-up about your new service.

What about the start-up money? In addition to the cost of your promotion campaign, you'll have to invest in a personal computer—including printer. Purchase a fax machine from your first earnings. Not only will up-to-date communication equipment make your work much easier, it will also show your clients that they are being served in a professional manner. Other necessities include files and an efficient accounting system. Finally, consult established local professionals to assist you in complying with your community's licensing, bonding, and tax regulations.

43

Inventory Specialists Are in Demand

No one really knows when it began. Perhaps during the Stone Age. Ever since human beings started trading goods, they also enumerated reserve supplies. Was it possibly done daily at sunrise, midday, and sunset? Well, times change, and so have the counting methods. Today, people of all ages with a liking for methodical procedures, an ability for organizing people, and an appreciation for extra earnings are in charge of free-lance inventory-taking all year long.

Anyone who has ever worked for the wholesale or retail trade, or in the manufacturing field, has been aware of the importance of accurate inventory recordkeeping. But which businesses are looking for inventory specialists? Topping the list is a broad range of retail, discount, and some national chain stores. Then there are wholesale companies, warehouse sales clubs, and the many medium-sized and small manufacturers, as well as hospitals and large institutions. They all inventory their merchandise stock/supplies on a regular basis, some quarterly, others semiannually.

Admittedly, the latest telecommunications technology allows large corporations and national chain businesses to track their inventories nationwide by means of teletransaction computer (bar-code scanning), which eliminates the need for old-style inventory counting. Yet a variety of inventory-taking methods are still based on a combination of physical counting and computer-processing. Such combination inventory applies particularly to small manufacturers, wholesale and retail establishments, as well as institutions where physical stock counting is still done during off hours by groups of people working in teams of two to six individuals. By using inventory methods devised by their management, or accountants, businesses with a scaled-down office work force favor outside assistance for the tedious work of stock counting. This is a matter of economics, for personnel overtime payments generally far exceed the payments to outside specialists who move in with a working crew.

Bear in mind, the client will dictate the inventory format. You, the inventory service owner, will be informed about the counting method and recordkeeping to which you and your crew must adhere. On the other hand, it is up to you to assemble the inventory-counting crew and to keep an accurate record of each crew member's working hours. The crew size will depend on the extent of the assignment.

A crew member's qualifications should include ability to count merchandise accurately, dependability, physical fitness, and availability at odd hours, such as evenings to night hours and weekends.

In recent years a new twist has been added to inventory crew hiring. To keep the cost contained and to give charitable organizations a fund-raising opportunity, inventory specialists now frequently recruit members of churches, charitable and civic organizations for off-hours inventory work. The recruits volunteer their time to raise money either for the growth of their own organization or for community social projects. The hiring is generally negotiated between the inventory service owner and the group leader of the volunteers.

And how do you prepare the crew for their work? Prior to the scheduled inventory taking, arrange through the group leader to meet with the volunteer group. Talk to them about the meeting place, timetable, counting procedure, work breaks, and snacking. More businesses now furnish hand-held and -operated counting equipment, which must also be thoroughly demonstrated to the inventory takers.

Contract negotiations with the client must include the extent of the assignment, applied work method, timetable, crew size, and compensation. To arrive at the quoted service fee, add anywhere from 20 to 35 percent to the hourly pay of each crew member. This percentage over and above the crew payment should adequately compensate you for your time, effort, and any expenses. For example, a $3.50-per-hour-plus-percentage cost per inventory taker will have any businessperson look favorably at outside inventory taking.

When utilizing volunteer crews, it has been customary for the client to send a compensation check in the amount of the crew's total working hours directly to the volunteers' institution or organization. The additional percentage amount will be paid to you, the inventory service. Of course, arrangements can be altered to suit individual preferences and situations.

With the help of an introductory letter and a printed circular, promote your new service by personally contacting the businesses described above. Point out the flexible scheduling, service expediency, and the obvious economic advantage over any other type of inventory taking. To further promote the service, contact local business associations and place an occasional classified ad in your area's business papers.

Your public library has a number of books available that detail currently favored inventory procedures. To stay abreast of today's methods, study a few books recommended for the retail trade. Familiarize yourself with local licensing, bonding, and tax regulations, and have an established accountant devise an appropriate accounting system.

44

Collection Agent: Opportunity for Former Accountants

Picture from a distant past: If it ever happened, it happened to a neighbor or casual acquaintance, of course—a collection agent impetuously knocking at the front door, demanding an overdue payment! Today, debt collection is as widespread as ever, but the methods are very different from those used in years past.

Third-party debt collecting can become a respectable, challenging, profitable home-based business for a qualified individual. Does operating a small collection service interest you? It's a worthwhile objective for which experience in the credit-managing field, combined with knowledge, efficiency, and professionalism, is indispensable.

Since the collection agent contacts debtors by mail, telephone, or personal interview, he or she must be able to get along with all kinds of people and to firmly control any kind of situation. It's not a particularly difficult or complex task to manage a small, or one-person office, or the local branch of a national chain collection concern, but ultimately it is the agent's qualifications that will determine success. Bear in mind, there is a notable difference between having once been employed in the credit business field and striking out on your own.

In larger communities with an active economy, the outlook for debt collection services should be promising. The American consumer's ever-increasing use of credit and the resulting problems for credit grantors in collecting these debts create excellent opportunities for third-party collection firms. In a medium-sized community, clients may include small manufacturers, the extensive retail trade, financial institutions, professional services, even government agencies.

Nowadays, new collection services can specialize in a particular client field. Notice, for instance, that during the past decade a growing number of collection agents focused their attention exclusively on the debt collection needs of the expanding health-care industry. Besides hospitals and other health-care institutions, clients may be solicited among physicians, dentists, and veterinarians.

As far as financial investment is concerned, you will need to pay rent on an office if you decide to establish your operation outside your home. Select an office close to the location of your major client (e.g., large medical center and surrounding professional medical buildings). During the business planning stage, you will have to consider investing in a personal computer and business-related software. The advantages of a computerized service system are numerous: it steps up productivity, trims expenses, and gives you instant access to the multitude of data processed in a collection office. You may also have to connect to clients' on-line accounts systems.

Have well-prepared printed material on hand when you begin to solicit clients by direct mail, advertising, or personal calls. The promotional material should explain your procedures, your commission scale, your planned remittance and trust accounts. (The American Collectors Association urges collection agents to set up a separate trust fund at his/her bank for moneys collected from clients.) Also cultivate good relations with prospective and new clients. Referrals by satisfied customers will contribute to a healthy growth of your new business.

With new federal laws now being imposed on this highly regulated professional field, it is imperative to seek the counsel of a competent attorney (specializing in business and credit law). In addition to legal counsel, a reputable accountant and insurance professional can safely navigate you through multiple federal, state, and municipal requirements concerning licensing, record-keeping, bonding, and personal liabilities.

If you seriously consider a collection venture, your first step should be to contact the American Collectors Association, Inc., P.O. Box 39106, Minneapolis, MN 55439; (612) 926-6547. Their free pamphlets are listed below.

Suggested Reading

American Collectors Association. *Careers in Collections.* Minneapolis, 1988. (Order from American Collectors Association.)

———. *Starting and Managing a Collection Service.* Minneapolis, 1988. (Order from American Collectors Association.)

45

Arts-Crafts Interest + Sales Ability = Effective Agent/Broker

Wasn't it just yesterday that you closely examined the roughened texture of handmade pottery and exquisitely crafted wood mosaic wallhangings? And numerous other well-styled, imaginative craft items caught your attention. As a matter of fact, you were impressed by the creative and inventive atmosphere at this shopping-mall craft show. Wouldn't it be fascinating to get involved as a sales agent for such remarkable products?

Well, nothing stops you from pursuing an enjoyable part-time business in this field. You don't even have to be an artisan or craftsperson. If you're a commonsense businessperson, and possess organizational talent, a substantial income over the years can be your reward.

Not everywhere, but in many parts of the country, scores of capable artisans and craftspersons turn out a huge amount of products. These products include paintings, pottery, leather goods, decorative hand-woven textiles, handcrafted custom jewelry, wood carvings, metal and wire sculptures. To scout for products, visit as many indoor and outdoor events in your area as you possibly can. Keep your eyes open and focus your attention on product quality and originality to determine an item's market appeal and salability. It's quite possible that an appealing, unique and attractively priced item hasn't been brought to the attention of the buying public because the person who made it lacks business experience. This is where your sales talent will play a decisive role.

As a go-between for the artisan/craftsperson and the urban or suburban retailer, specialty store and gift shop owner, you can become the link between the two parties, to the benefit of both. The agent's commission generally ranges from 35 to 50 percent of the producer's asking price.

When exploring the arts and crafts market in your area, apply the criteria discussed above. Introduce yourself with business card and references. Contact and obtain information from artisans/craftspersons who meet established standards; then keep records of interviews and furnished product information. An essential piece of information concerns productivity—whether the supplier can guarantee a steady stream of those items that happen to become good sellers.

After you have established a rapport with a diverse group of artisans/craftspersons, begin to personally approach retailers, specialty store proprietors, as well as institutional, hotel, and airport gift shops, with carefully selected product samples. Be prepared to leave these samples with the stores for a certain period of time. During the winter and spring holiday seasons, when hospitals, clubs, and churches hold their bazaars, add to the list of prospects these organizations' fund-raising committees. If necessary, make them an offer to sell the items on a consignment basis.

It is of great importance to select quality and imaginative products with sales appeal, as well as to keep meticulous records on merchandise that changes hand from one party to another. A professional approach in dealings with both parties is essential. You should also jot down retailers' reactions and determine the acceptance of the suggested pricing.

A distinct advantage of becoming an agent/broker is the low financial investment. This helps compensate for the fact that the business moves at a slow pace in the beginning. You must be willing to let a merchant test the market first, for you and the offered products are unknown to him or her. The working relationship between you and the store owner will improve at the moment he or she begins to sell the products offered. What may start out as consignment transactions will gradually develop into wholesale purchasing by store owners.

And once you have won the confidence of both supplier and dealer, the trade will definitely begin to increase.

Some states and communities have strict licensing laws for bona fide brokerage services. Clarify all legal details with established local professionals (attorney, accountant, insurance professional), who can counsel you on service-related requirements. The guidelines in this chapter can readily be applied to the art market, if this should be your preferred field. To become the liaison between artists and gallery owners can be equally rewarding.

Suggested Reading

Long, Steve, and Cindy Long. *You Can Make Money from Your Arts and Crafts*. Scotts Valley, Calif.: Mark Publications, 1988.

46

Be an Interior Decorating Consultant to a Special Clientele

You have done it many times—that is, turned an ordinary living space into an interior showcase! Perhaps, just recently, you have won acclaim by cleverly blending lush-colored wildflower upholstery patterns with maize floor covering, opulent glass tables, and mercury-colored window blinds framed by lambrequins upholstered in a complementary color.

If you have the talent to develop client-pleasing interior decorating schemes, by all means, capitalize on your skills, experience, and taste. An interior decorating consultant's free-lance work includes coordination of paint colors, wall and floor coverings, window treatments, and furniture arrangements. Such a service can be not only financially rewarding but satisfying as well, for you will help people create an enjoyable living environment in their homes.

When you establish yourself as a self-employed consultant, consider focusing on a special clientele: the ever-increasing number of mature citizens over the age of fifty. Many of them contemplate a change of residence, thus giving up a larger home for more compact living quarters, be it a house, condominium, or apartment. It's the beginning of a new chapter in their lives. At that point, homeowners are confronted with a multitude of decisions. Most must part with large furniture pieces. So they welcome professional help to coordinate the shell of their new quarters with newly acquired furnishings that will reflect their new life-style. Among this sizable segment of the population, you will find a multitude of appreciative prospects.

A consultant's skills include know-how in areas ranging from furnishings, textiles, and floor coverings to window treatments, wall coverings, and paints. In this profession, it is essential to stay informed at all times about the latest decorating materials, techniques, trends, and colors. To update your knowledge and fine-tune your skills, consult a variety of interior decorating books and periodicals available at your public library and bookstores. Or take a course at a community college or adult education institution where local professional designers often teach both the basics and specialized subjects.

If you desire work experience before starting your own independent service, you may want to explore temporary part-time work at a reputable home furnishings establishment. Quality furniture stores, leading wallpaper and paint centers, and specialty stores for window dressings are always looking for temporary personnel with decorating experience.

As a consultant, you should specialize in the area of your past training and work experience. For example, your future service may concentrate on coordinating paint, wallpaper, and carpet. Or you may want to focus on furniture, providing assistance with purchasing and with arrangements of pieces and accessories. Others may want to utilize their know-how in window treatments and bedroom accessories. And then there are those who wish to use their creative talents to develop complete decorating schemes for homes and apartments.

Consult **MYRA**

800-1110

★ SPECIALIZING IN SENIOR INTERIORS
★ TRUST HER IMPECCABLE TASTE!

You can operate your service from your attractively decorated home. At all times, cultivate good relations with various reputable home furnishings stores in your area. You will depend on their cooperation and supply of material samples, and, in return, you may refer your clients to them for purchases.

Your service fees should follow locally established rates, usually set by design professionals. However, your remuneration should be below the charges of a degreed designer if you do not have academic credentials in this field.

Your quotation to the client should include the job fee, based on estimated number of work hours, plus expenses. Any job estimate should be prepared with great care. It makes good business sense to present the client with a simple work contract, spelling out the extent of your consultation work, the quoted fee, plus payment date.

Until you can count on word-of-mouth referrals, publicize the new service in your neighborhood papers. You can also spread word through real estate brokers, Welcome Wagon organizations, and home-building contractors. Good rapport with contractors can result in some model-suite decorating with the cooperation of local retailers of home furnishings. Those who want to target a mature clientele should contact managers of retirement communities, developers of the now popular retirement condominiums, and managers of upscale senior citizens' apartment buildings.

Lastly, look into the zoning, licensing, and tax regulations, as well as bonding requirements in your community. Established local professionals should counsel you on forming your service business.

Suggested Reading

Lant, Jeffrey L. *The Consultant's Kit.* 2d ed. Cambridge, Mass.: JLA Publications, 1981.

47

Special Person Wanted: Consumer Rights Agent

How could I ever forget my former neighbor, Mr. Lamento? He lived in a continual state of consumer misery. He drove his creaking jeep for ten years. It was a lemon from day one. Mr. Lamento's home air conditioner failed the first week, never worked efficiently ever since. And the contractor who poured the cement in his driveway missed the last workday, leaving him with a bumpy surface.

What Mr. Lamento needed was a consumer rights agent. Have you ever successfully fought for consumer rights, either for yourself or for others? If you have been previously affiliated with a consumer action group, or with a local or state consumer affairs office, the valuable knowledge you acquired is very much in demand today.

Requisites for this rewarding community-oriented service are the ability to solve problems, the determination to get results, and the assertiveness to articulate verbal or written consumer complaints. Not only do such individuals enjoy a challenge, but they frequently rush forth whenever Joe Doe's basic rights are violated.

But is there enough business around to make such an activity profitable? Any medium-sized city or county area should offer hundreds of prospective clients in need of service. Think of all the consumers who become bogged down when entangled in merchandise or service complaints with manufacturers, merchants, service firms, health professionals, or government agencies. They need someone to turn to for assistance with legitimate complaints.

If you contemplate becoming a consumer rights agent, begin your preparations by doing research in your local main library. The volume of literature on the subject of consumerism is impressive. Study the latest approaches and techniques for getting industry and business to respond quickly to customer complaints. Familiarize yourself with the numerous agencies on local, state, and federal levels that now assist everyone who has a legitimate merchandise or service claim. Then contact local private consumer action groups or semiofficial consumer affairs agencies. They can direct you to additional information sources. The purpose is to become thoroughly acquainted with the methods that have been successfully utilized by prominent consumer advocates in the past. Study the success stories. You will discover how to cut red tape by channeling a given claim to the right individual or department head.

Additional preparations include an examination of your community's licensing, tax, and bonding regulations. Counseling by competent local professionals (attorney, certified public accountant, insurance professional) will help you in this regard.

The next step should be to develop your own guidelines and checklist for prospective clients. Any action on a client's behalf requires the gathering of all facts relevant to the claim. Start designing your own questionnaire to maintain a permanent fact sheet in your client's file. Discuss the forthcoming correspondence procedure; for example, where responses to the claim should be sent, to you or to the client. Also, record the client's preferences.

Prior to commencing the service, have the client sign a simple contract. This document should include the type of compensation (refund, replacement, adjustment) the client is seeking. Also specify your fee, which should reimburse you adequately for your work and expenses.

At the promotional end, have a flyer or folder printed, as well as a boldly designed business card. The latter can be tacked to bulletin boards of food markets and other public gathering places. Don't overlook the potential of larger apartment buildings, civic clubs, credit union offices, and local consumer groups.

To get started, it will be necessary to place some classified ads in your local daily newspaper(s) and weekly suburban publications. Enlist the help of the papers' ad writers or the agency that will design your promotional material. They can suggest effective four- or five-line ads. Each ad should strongly appeal to those in need of help to settle consumer complaints. State that your service is available at an affordable fee, and include your telephone number for service inquiries. Test your advertising by keeping a record of how many inquiries each ad generates. Sharpen the wording if the consumer response is unsatisfactory. Study other classified ads and learn from them.

After successful conclusion of several consumer claim cases, consider two more ideas to generate business for the consumer rights agent: first, initiating advertised evening lecturers on consumer rights and drawing flocks of people with claim problems to the lecture hall (similar to the lectures of financial planners); second, passing on news items on successfully concluded claim cases to the local newspaper(s), thus encouraging reluctant consumers to contact the agent on behalf of their own merchandise or service claims.

Suggested Reading

Bloomstein, Morris J. *Consumer's Guide to Fighting Back*. New York: Dodd, Mead, 1976.

Charell, Ralph. *How I Turn Ordinary Complaints into Thousands of Dollars*. New York: Stein and Day, 1973.

Dorfman, John. *Consumer Tactics Manual*. New York: Atheneum, 1980.

48

Looking for a Challenge? Become a Convention Assistant

Picture this scenario: Friday night—a thousand miles away from home—Jack P. has arrived at a convention hotel after a three-hour flight delay. He plunges immediately into the preparations for the Saturday morning sales meeting, the organization of which is his responsibility. No time to catch a bite to eat. It's getting late, and he begins to perspire as not one, but three, equipment breakdowns occur and he realizes there's a shortage of printed materials for the meeting. Isn't there any helping hand around?

It would have been a great relief if Jack could have relied on a local aide (convention assistant) with connections to area specialists and supply sources that provide services around the clock.

Does the service of a convention assistant appeal to you? You might consider it if you're living in a city or resort town that attracts brisk convention business, and if you're looking for an exciting, challenging, and financially rewarding part-time activity. The primary requirements are organizational skills, business savvy, resourcefulness, and familiarity with all aspects of the area's business community. Good relations with the local convention trade, as well as a wide range of service businesses, are imperative. Other essential qualifications are integrity and dependability.

The functions of a convention assistant are manifold. First of all, the assistant is an aide to out-of-town convention organizers, business executives, and exhibitors in all convention-related arrangements. Among other tasks, the convention assistant should be able to communicate effectively with local repair services in case of equipment breakdowns, and with supply sources in the event of an unexpected need for specific materials. Additionally, specialists and laborers for after-hours services must be located, and product demonstrations for out-of-town exhibitors must be finalized. Finally, the assistant serves as liaison to local convention tour services. If these are unavailable, the assistant should be in a position to arrange desired sightseeing tours with local tour operators and transportation businesses.

Begin your preparations by establishing impeccable references which will be requested by the out-of-town corporations and organizations you will be serving. Seek counsel from local professionals about pertinent business requirements. Instead of looking to the library for relevant literature, rely on the local convention business community for broadening and updating your knowledge in this field. Keep your eyes and ears open when making the rounds of convention hotels and exhibition centers. Such hubs of tourist and convention activities will prove to be extremely useful information sources.

While making contacts within the convention community, you may encounter other free-lancing convention assistants. In a large city there is always room for another enterprising man or woman with fresh and creative marketing ideas. I recently met one such individual, who has established a thriving business as a convention assistant. This former sales representative cherishes his new activities and charges fees ranging from $100 to $150 per day plus expenses, depending on the extent of the assignment.

The service promotion should focus on advertisements in local publications that target the convention/tourist business and should include a listing in the Yellow Pages. With an attractive business card and a printed folder in hand, you can spread the word of your service through personal contacts with the hospitality trade, convention promoters, and exhibition centers. They may even be willing to furnish listings of organizations and corporations that have conventions in the planning stage.

49

||||➡ ⬅||||

Eager to Attend Auctions? Enjoy Being a Representative

Nowadays, a great deal of treasured objects from the past are being acquired through auctions; coins, stamps, artwork, antiques, oriental rugs, and furniture. It's a fact that many of these auctions are held on weekdays during regular business hours, and in large metropolitan areas two or more important auctions are occasionally scheduled concurrently. This poses problems for the numerous individuals who have a keen interest in collecting objects of value, on the one hand, and a tight weekday work or travel schedule, on the other. An auction representative can come to the rescue. He or she does the bidding for the client/collector, when he or she is unable to attend, or stays for the duration of the often lengthy bidding event if the collector must leave.

When contemplating this service activity, take into consideration whether you have a business or personal knowledge of collectibles. Also consider whether you can observe the highest ethical standards. This type of service must be built on trust, honesty, and reliability. Flawless references are essential. It is of utmost importance that you perform your service as an unattached, independent businessperson. That is, you cannot associate yourself with any member of the auction-holding sales party. Remember, you must enjoy your client's confidence and assure him or her that you represent no other client at the same sales event.

You are bidding exclusively for one client and must adhere to his or her precise bidding instructions. These instructions must specify the minimum and maximum amount the client wishes to spend for the desired object(s).

Before establishing a fee schedule, first investigate the charges of other auction representatives in your area or neighboring larger cities. It is customary to charge a flat fee that covers time and expenses. Some representatives I have talked to set their minimum fee at $75. The flat fee should increase considerably when bidding on items of substantial value or when bidding for several items. A flat fee also rules out any bidding manipulations on the part of the representative.

You can launch the promotion of your service with classified ads in the appropriate section of your local or area newspapers. Further, with business card and a well-designed flyer, introduce your service to respectable art/antique dealers, interior designers, and local collectors' clubs. Also take time to locate and call personally on your area's leading private art collectors. This diverse group comprises business executives, health and law professionals, educators, and others. Many of these busy individuals have served, or are currently serving, on the board of trustees of museums, art institutions, performing arts and educational organizations.

Finally, review your area's license, tax, and bonding regulations, and consult a local attorney, accountant, and insurance professional for guidance on complying with all service requirements.

Suggested Reading

Roberts, Ralph. *Auction Action! A Survival Companion for Any Auction Goer*. Blue Ridge Summit, Pa.: Tab Books, 1986.

50

||||▶ ◀||||

Utilize Your Accounting Skills: Set Up a Recordkeeping Business

Have you managed a business, or worked in bookkeeping or in accounting? Training and experience in the business administration field are highly valued assets in today's marketplace. Utilizing these skills can make your coming years challenging and financially rewarding.

In case you are retired, staying professionally active and augmenting your retirement income will not only ensure your continuing involvement with the community but, at the same time, render a valuable service to small businesses.

Such a venture will allow you to control your time by taking on as few or as many clients as will comfortably fit your established work schedule. You also have the

option of obtaining a franchise from a national accounting and tax service that wishes to branch out in your
area. See Appendix B for information on how to order
the latest *Directory of Franchising Organizations*.

In almost any community setting there is a sizable
market for recordkeeping services of any size. The
number of small businesses in need of assistance is
steadily on the rise. Bound by law, even the smallest
business must regularly file a variety of reports pertinent to its business classification. Further, there are tax
returns to be computed; withholding taxes to be paid;
cash, bank, and inventory records to be maintained; in
addition to taking care of daily ledger entries. Despite
the increasing paperwork, only a minority of small
firms have full-time office workers. Most small businesses, including the mushrooming independent networking marketers, depend on regular outside help.

The original equipment investment in this service
field is moderate. You can convert a room in your home
into a small office by adding a desk, reliable telephone
system, typewriter, calculating equipment, and an expandable filing system. You may want to reinvest your
early profits in a personal computer and software. Up-
to-date equipment will help you serve your clients in a
professional and efficient manner, enabling you to tailor
your recordkeeping methods to a diverse small business
clientele, and enhancing your chances of being competitive in the marketplace.

At first, client solicitation will occupy most of your
time. You can attract your first clients through classified
ads in local papers and commercial periodicals. Engage
a small or quick print shop for your printing needs, such
as business cards and flyers. The shop itself will be-

come a source for locating new business prospects. Early in your promotional efforts introduce yourself to the local office of the Small Business Administration and your local SCORE chapter (Service Corps of Retired Executives). Then, armed with cover letter and well-defined circular, call on owners or managers of small businesses and service firms in your immediate location. Finally, if needed, consider a mailing to managers of retail stores, car dealers, small hotels, motels, inns, restaurants, food services.

Other potential client sources are services and trades, such as barber shops, beauty salons, service stations, car repair shops, electronic repair services, the various decorating retailers and service companies, printing and engraving firms, small building contractors, independent truckers, and the ever-growing health-care field. Small manufacturers, metal fabricators, mold and die makers, and plastic molders, to name a few, all depend on recordkeeping assistance. Lastly, tap the daily expanding pool of self-employed marketers representing the surging direct-selling companies. These local marketers can be reached through networking and marketing organizations and their publications. Or, by keeping an eye on their classified sales ads in local newspapers, you can also approach the marketers through direct mail.

Before finalizing a competitive fee structure, investigate current charges of existing recordkeeping service firms in your area; client charges are mostly settled on a monthly basis. It is also essential to contact a competent attorney, as well as insurance professional, and request counseling on all matters of community and state business requirements. Have your legal counsel draft a client contract.

Suggested Reading

Small Business Administration. See pertinent pamphlets listed in Appendix B.

Small Business Reporter. *Establishing an Accounting Practice*. SBR 119. San Francisco, 1988. (Order from Small Business Reporter, Bank of America, Dept. 3631, P.O. Box 37000, San Francisco, CA 94137.)

————. *Financial Records for Small Business*. SBR 128. San Francisco, 1988. (Order from Small Business Reporter.)

51

Mail-order Selling: A Venture for the Knowledgeable

A future electronic shopping-by-computer revolution? Sounds great! With push-button ease via your telecomputer, you can secure anything from a price-slashed Alpine ski machine to a couple of jars of miracle-promising antiwrinkle creme, without physically plunging into a postholiday sales battle at your favorite department store. The computerized banking you do afterward may be less gratifying.

Yet this publicized simplified shopping concept appears not to be in our immediate future, at least not for the first half of the nineties. In the meantime, turn your attention again to your favorite mail-order and direct-response catalogs. Their successful selling is likely to continue—for now. Numerous enterprising men and women in their midtwenties all the way to the seventies enthusiastically take advantage of the ongoing mail-order mania. They join the trade and cash in on its wealth.

The astounding advances of even some small mail-order entrepreneurs, however, require a word of caution. The avalanche of classified magazine advertisements and countless tabloid stories create the impression that mail-order selling is a sure "get-rich-quick" scheme which anyone can pursue. The fact: it is not a "become-affluent-overnight" business pursuit. Early substantial monetary rewards are rare, and reasonable investment returns are hard earned. Only experienced individuals have a chance to cash in on the boom. For the uninitiated, this business is not without dangerous risks. Only a modest but well-organized start, long hours of hard work, and intensive market study and testing may lead to expansion and success.

Let me begin by clarifying some basic terms of the trade:

Mail order is a method of marketing products that have been presented to consumers by means of media advertisements or direct mail (letter, brochure, flyer). Both means, advertisements and consumer mailings, generally feature a blank order form, which the buying consumer fills out and returns with the specified payment to the mail-order firm. The company then must ship the ordered merchandise to the consumer within a six-week period.

The mail-order entrepreneur is bound by Federal

Trade Commission regulations to offer the customer a product-return money-back guarantee. Also, if the shipping period is to exceed six weeks, the entrepreneur must notify the customer of the expected shipping date, and give him/her the option of order cancellation.

Direct mail is a method of advertising a product(s) via letter, flyer, catalog. Consumer names for direct mailing are obtained from purchased mailing lists. The latter are sold by mailing-list traders who specialize in an abundance of listings for any purpose imaginable. It is noteworthy, though, that a purchased mailing list can be utilized for a onetime mailing only.

Direct marketing refers to a range of promotional methods including network marketing, telemarketing, TV advertising, and mailing of product discount coupons.

One of the reasons the mail-order business attracts so many venturesome men and women is that it can be started as a home-based hobby with minimum overhead and family assistance. For a modest beginning, a minimum capital of a few thousand dollars appears to be adequate. While operating the business at one's own pace, one can gain valuable experience and break even or perhaps make a small profit. At this phase, reinvesting in additional advertising is a wise move.

Three factors are crucial in this business:

First, the *product(s)* to be sold must be carefully chosen with market know-how. Such products range from novelties and quaint home products to handmade goods and trendy fashion pieces. Another lucrative field is the hobby-craft market, which may include anything from unique handcrafts, coins, and new-age crystals to popular collectibles of any kind: dolls, wall plates, even thimbles. (The equally successful mail-order "information" selling is discussed in Chapter 61.)

Second, the *merchandise sources* must be thoroughly investigated and the profit margin of each item must be carefully calculated to avoid losses and to remain competitive.

Third, the *advertising* methods must be diligently studied and carefully chosen. After deciding where and how long to run the ads, the purchased advertising constitutes the largest expense. This applies to the purchase of ad space in daily newspapers or in weekly/monthly periodicals, as well as to direct-letter mailing.

The subject of successful advertising is too extensive to be discussed within this limited format. A few important points: It is of utmost importance to select the appropriate type of media to get the message to the targeted consumer, and to purchase the most suitable mailing lists. Experiment with the advertising message and the ad's timing to maximize results. Attention must also be given to coding ad coupons (to identify the publication[s] generating responses from consumers) and to consumer appeal of the printed promotional materials.

Mail-order industry studies indicate that the response rate from either media advertising or direct mail can be as low as 2 percent but rarely exceeds 6 to 7 percent. This necessitates sharp price calculations. If you are a novice in the mail-order business, investigate your area's legal requirements. You must select a company name for registration, look into existing zoning laws, and obtain a vendor's license. Because you will engage in interstate commerce, you should be prepared to collect sales taxes for other states in addition to your home state. Counseling by established local professionals (attorney, accountant, insurance professional) is mandatory in this ever-widening business field. You may also request information from the Direct Marketing Association, 11 West 42nd Street, New York, NY 10036; (212) 768-7277.·

Suggested Reading

Federal Trade Commission. *Mail Order Rule*. Washington, D.C.: Government Printing Office, 1986. (Order from Superintendent of Documents, U.S. Printing Office, Washington, DC 20402 or its regional branch office.)

Hoge, Cecil C., Sr. *Mail Order Moonlighting*. Berkeley, Calif.: Ten Speed Press, 1976.

Small Business Administration. *Selling by Mail Order*. (See Appendix B for details on how to order this pamphlet.)

52

IIII▶ ◀IIII

Popular Direct-sales/
Network Marketing

Did you recently scan your newspaper's employment ads? Which ones caught your attention? The ones offering "sales opportunities with unlimited earning potential"? Naturally, you were curious about such tempting offers and responded. When you learned about the particulars—be honest now—were you encouraged or disappointed?

Let's make it clear that the current direct-sales and multilevel marketing business explosion, also called network marketing, is not for those who are timid, uninitiated, inefficient, or unteachable! Yet motivated, determined women and men with a genuine liking for people, frequently experienced in sales, marketing, or teaching, have proven that rapid advances are possible in this unique, booming, billion-dollar industry.

Examining these publicized opportunities, we discover that newspaper ad slogans generally stress "independence," which means: working hours of your own choosing. Next are the "high earnings" promises, touting the potential for a six-figure annual income. Finally, "low investment," which translates into mandatory purchases of distributor sales kit, product samples, one to two months' product inventory, and promotional materials.

At it turns out, direct-sales companies compensate their sales force on a sales commission-only basis, and most of these hard-working associates take home a more realistic commission of several hundred dollars per month. These modest commission checks are the result of diligent efforts of door-to-door, party-plan, and direct-mail selling, and recruiting of new distributors. Add to these efforts prompt product deliveries to customers who value personal service.

According to statistics, the self-employed sales force of the direct-sales industry in this country now boasts several million individuals; and the numbers are steadily rising. The majority of these independent salespersons are women. Industry data further indicate that the drop-out rate of new recruits is high. Apparently, many new marketers, as the sales associates are called, are not aware of the performance expectations placed upon them.

The direct-sales product lines now cover anything from health care to cleaning products, from cookware to cosmetics, from fashion merchandise and custom jewelry to novel toys and craft supplies. Whatever the product(s), the direct-sales company expects you to test-market it and your sales techniques within your extended family, circle of friends, and with co-workers before venturing into the neighborhood with door-to-door selling.

Party-plan selling is another sales strategy promoted by many direct-sales companies with multiple products. First, recruit a host or hostess among friends or neigh-

Network Marketing Can Be Profitable

Can an independent, fortyish woman, who grew up in rural Alaska, become a promising network marketing success in the Midwest? Yes. Sandi Smith is the living proof. After nursing herself back to health from a devastating car accident, this brave and inspiring individual resigned from her secure position as a legal secretary to take the plunge into a direct-selling venture, marketing a nutritional health product she highly values. A year later, this likable and articulate marketer enlightens new customers in a caring manner and recruits, educates, trains, and supervises new distributors within the multilevel marketing structure of her direct-sales distributorship. The rewards: a steady stream of new customers and a devoted distributor corps that grows and grows—and so does Sandi's bank account.

bors; then demonstrate the product(s) on a weekday evening in the host's or hostess's home before an invited group of friends. Any meeting expenses are borne by you. This type of selling is time-consuming. It entails mailing invitations, planning the presentation and entertainment, transporting product samples, recruiting new distributors, and, finally, seeing to follow-ups and order deliveries. During the first weeks of your sales activities you are generally aided by your sponsoring mar-

keter. You are also expected to regularly attend
company training/pep rallies and company-sponsored
sales seminars which will make additional demands on
your time and finances.

Soon you will concentrate on assembling a sales team
that will multiply itself—the new recruits will, in turn,
locate more new recruits. Your sales commissions will
also multiply, increasing in direct ratio to your and your
team's sales results. You are obligated to guide and supervise the sales activities of your new team members.

Your door-to-door, party, and direct-mail selling can
produce a net sales commission anywhere from 8 to 40
percent, depending on the company, product, and sales
volume.

If this challenging sales field appeals to you, thoroughly examine the company and the product(s) before
signing on as a sales associate:

- Find out whether the company has a first-rate marketing plan with worthy incentives and a beneficial
  and fair distribution system. Carefully study the
  company's multilevel marketing structure, which
  varies from company to company. Does it favor
  only the top layer of associates, or is it structured to
  give all marketers an equal chance and share?
- Question members of the sales force, or seek advice
  from outside veterans in the field.
- Determine whether the product or product line is
  unique and fulfills universal needs, whether it is
  geared to profitable repeat sales, and whether you
  feel comfortable about publicly associating yourself
  with it.

Final words of caution: you have to meet quotas and sales objectives to get ahead in this business. And note that your actual financial investments generally exceed the original projection. Be prepared to have all accruing expenses covered until you receive the first commission check, which is sometimes slow in coming. Lastly, an essential requirement is reliable, spacious transportation to call on customers, to transport demonstration supplies, and to make product deliveries.

In your home you should designate a suitable area to handle the business paperwork. The investment in a personal computer will eventually become necessary. Your residence must also be suitable for the storage of product samples and merchandise inventory.

Your promotional efforts should include leaving company literature at prospects' homes and at apartment doors. Also make good use of bulletin boards at shopping malls, food markets, beauty salons, Laundromats, churches, civic centers, and credit union offices. Mailing letters to tenants of large apartment buildings is also a successful marketing tool but classified advertising is usually not expected at the beginning of your sales career.

The direct-sales company and your sponsoring associate will keep you posted about the need for any legal counsel, and about license and sales tax requirements in your area. If you strike out independently, have reputable local professionals advise you on all service-related regulations.

For your convenience, a selected listing of direct-sales and multilevel marketing companies appears in Appendix A. You may also contact the Direct Selling Association, 1776 K Street, NW, Suite 600, Washington, DC 20006 and the Multi-Level Marketing International Association (MLMIA), 119 Stanford, Irvine, CA 92715.

Suggested Reading

Scott, Gini Graham. *Strike It Rich in Personal Selling*. New York: Avon Books, 1985.
Tartaglia, Gary. *Shattered Dreams: How to Avoid Costly Mistakes in Multi-Level Marketing*. Cleveland: Calaciura, 1985.

53

Any Linguists Around? Form a Translation Service

All right, you admit, you really haven't had opportunities lately to utilize the other language you can speak fluently. Do you realize that today, more than ever before, being bilingual or multilingual is a valuable marketable asset? The emphasis is on fluency—speaking, reading, and writing.

Admittedly, the commercial use of foreign languages is a specialized field. In the forefront of the steadily rising demand are manufacturers, trade and political organizations, as well as educational and scientific institutions. With the heavy emphasis placed on the accelerating export-import trade, in the nineties and beyond even more medium and small U.S. manufacturers, exporters, and importers will become participants in interdependent global trading.

Unlike the multinational corporations, which employ their own linguistic staff, small and first-time exporters frequently look for outside assistance to handle their foreign-language business correspondence or technical translations. These businesses seem to be more comfortable contracting with a small, local personalized service than with a faraway, big-city firm.

In addition, there are professionals in each community who require occasional major language translations. They work in marketing and public relations agencies, travel agencies, organizations with foreign ties, even churches, large health-care institutions, and others.

Currently, demand for the Russian, Japanese, Chinese, and Korean languages has intensified. As the U.S. export field stretches to the far south of the Americas, to all parts of Europe, and to the Middle East, languages such as Spanish, Portuguese, French—even Arabic—experience a resurgence. Other traditional European languages, like German, Italian, Polish, and the Scandinavian tongues, are still widely used in international trade relations.

You can capitalize on your own language skills by operating a low-investment, home-based translation service. In the beginning, it doesn't require more than basic office equipment, up-to-date reference books, and foreign-language dictionaries.

Introduce your services to exporting manufacturers, importers, and other businesses with ties to international trade. Names of prospective clients can be obtained from your area's export association and from state and local government agencies that promote exports. A list of professions with occasional translation needs begins on page 191.

Before setting up your fee schedule, contact existing translation services in your region and study their charges. Some translation jobs are based on hourly rates, others on per-page translations.

If you are a sales-oriented person, there are other opportunities you can seize. Does your community have a measurable ethnic population and are you part of it? If so, you can combine two valuable assets—offer your foreign-language communication skills to a variety of merchants/dealers (real estate, insurance, cars, appliances, electronic home equipment) who cater to foreign-born customers. In major cities with a diverse immigrant population, numerous success stories are circulating about prosperous foreign-language speaking salespersons. Immigrant families and naturalized citizens naturally gravitate toward sales personnel with whom they can transact a major purchase in their native tongue. With a good service reputation, you can build a loyal following.

Publicize your sales services on the bulletin board of the local international institute or other publicly funded agencies assigned to assist new immigrants. Contact with ethnic social clubs will also help spread the word about your service.

Investigate at county and municipal levels about licensing, bonding, and tax regulations for the intended service. Note that to serve the legal profession or a court of law, special requirements apply. Reputable local professionals can advise you on legal, accounting, and liability matters.

54

Good Connections in Foreign Countries? Look at These Opportunities

Wouldn't you enjoy regularly traveling to countries whose language you speak? There must have been times when you thought: How can I best utilize my bilingual background and foreign contacts? Or how do my language skills fit into a home-based service business including foreign travel? Here they are—splendid opportunities for qualified naturalized citizens, and for those who can capitalize on their roots and connections to other countries.

The qualifications? Well, you should be physically fit, people-oriented, and fluent in at least one foreign language. Also, you must thrive on challenges and establish flawless references.

One of the popular choices is to set up a *foreign buying service*. This is particularly suited to individuals who once or twice annually visit a country to which they still have close family or business ties. But what should you buy and import? Consider the country's specialties. For example, some excel in specialty apparel, like silk dresses or robes, others in tweed jackets, woolen blazers, knitwear. Some nations are known for their quality leather goods, trendy costume jewelry, exquisite linens, or quaint home decorations.

Here at home, we find an increasing number of quality- or fashion-conscious consumers willing to pay for out-of-the-ordinary items. News about unique, fashionable, or quality merchandise travels fast. And acceptance of the products will assure you a stream of enthusiastic new and repeat customers.

Your foreign merchandise sources must not only supply you with illustrated, English-language literature, but also be willing to expedite direct shipments to your customers. Your function is to obtain from your client size, style, and color choices, and prepayment, including shipping cost for direct shipment, so that you don't have to stock or warehouse the imports. Your compensation will be a percentage of the merchandise price. (You may have to test the market at an early stage before finalizing the pricing.)

As a *foreign representative*, you can become the link between small local retailers and foreign exporters, wholesalers, or manufacturers. Are you knowledgeable in a particular merchandise field? Your know-how might be of interest to area retailers willing to sell unique imported products. In steady demand are foreign antiques, novel handicrafts, woven decorative items, Oriental rugs, and coins.

During your travels, it is important to cultivate useful personal contacts with either foreign wholesalers or small manufacturers. Most foreign producers are anxious to find a U.S. market opening; they welcome any trustworthy, knowledgeable coordinator.

Check with your local U.S. customs authorities for the license and import duty regulations, as well as import procedures mandatory in your state. Many communities have export/import advisory boards affiliated with the local chamber of commerce. They will gladly assist you in your new endeavor. Moreover, make good use of the free service of your local SCORE office (Service Corps of Retired Executives). Many chapters have staff members with lifelong knowledge in import and export matters. By all means, take advantage of their know-how and recommendations of informative reading material.

And there is another type of service that has been pursued successfully by naturalized citizens, and others, with useful personal ties to other countries. Some call themselves *consultants*, others *representatives*. The individuals I contacted live in or close to larger cities with segments of foreign-born citizens and residents. Flawless references, demonstrated trustworthiness, and negotiation skills are essential qualifications for the service they perform. They give personalized assistance to foreign-born and native Americans of all ages who are engaged in pending, or forthcoming, legal transactions at foreign courts of law or with foreign authorities. The majority of cases involve bequests of some sort. For example, U.S. citizens may inherit part of, or may become sole heir to, an estate in a foreign country. Claiming an inheritance and settling other legal matters are not without complexity in any country.

Hank Keefer, a former multinational corporation executive, travels two or three times annually to Germany and Austria, where he acts as a liaison between American clients and, in bequest cases, the foreign probate courts or attorneys. While all legal aspects are handled by his clients' attorneys here in the States, Hank does the legwork in countries in which he speaks the language. His compensation consists of paid expenses plus a percentage fee of the total bequest claim. Occasionally, he finalizes more than one case during one overseas trip. Hank, and others in this field, enjoy their travels and consider their work challenging and rewarding. Such service can be carried out in any country that permits money and material transfers to foreign countries.

Prospective clients can be generated through ethnic social clubs, foreign legations (consulates), or law firms that serve a foreign-born clientele. Legal advisers, in particular, appreciate the work of bilingual representatives who do the actual legwork abroad. And most cases involve plenty of routine work outside the legal domain. Recommendations by the above sources are valuable assets in establishing a loyal clientele.

Professional counsel is mandatory for all the services described in this chapter. Therefore, contact a reputable attorney, accountant, and insurance professional who will assist you with local business regulations.

Suggested Reading

Green, Mary, and Stanley Gillmar. *How to Be an Importer and Pay for Your World Travel*. Berkeley, Calif.: Ten Speed Press, 1979.

Part V

Minibusiness Ideas for People with Teaching, Writing, and Travel Experience

55

▌▌▌➤ ◀▐▐▐

Art Shows Can Be Rewarding: Why Not Promote Them?

Locally made hand-woven wallhangings, pottery, sculptures, and paintings, abstract and traditional—are they plentiful in your community? Haven't the decorative arts always fascinated you? You may have been exposed to them through classroom teaching, the arts trade, or as a volunteer or docent at your local art museum. If you love the decorative arts, enjoy dealing with artists and artisans, and have good powers of persuasion, what can be more enjoyable and rewarding than promoting art shows? You can do this work on a part- or full-time basis, and earn a good income for years to come. You many even like to team up with an equally enthusiastic spouse of friend.

Even smaller communities offer opportunities for the art show promoter. You will be the link between talented local painters, sculptors, first-rate weavers, potters, and the interested buying public. Artists and artisans are always in need of attractive sales display settings. Therefore, they must be assured that their works will be presented in a stimulating surrounding that will tempt visitors to buy.

There are several ways to make financial arrangements with exhibiting artists. In the beginning, test the market with a flat exhibitor fee; this is the consensus of several successful promoters I have talked to. One of them works in tandem with his wife, a former art teacher. This resourceful couple has become widely known and respected. Another way of compensating the promoter is to reimburse a portion of the rental fee on the exhibit space plus provide a sales commission, both paid by the client, the exhibiting artist. The sales commission generally starts at the 10 percent level. This type of arrangement requires that you set a minimum charge. In other arrangements, the promoter splits equally his/her 50 percent of the sales revenue with the proprietor of the exhibition establishment, while the artist receives the remaining 50 percent. Such an arrangement requires tight control over sales figures.

Regardless of the kind of financial arrangement, a simple written contract with each exhibitor is in order. Furthermore, it is of vital importance to pay attention to the quality of the artistic works to be exhibited. It is mandatory to establish quality standards, which means, if necessary, turning down substandard products.

Several art show promoters agree that there is no shortage of artists/artisans who are looking for appropriate exposure to the public. Potential clients can be found through institutions of higher education, commercial art schools, art teachers, even the art supply trade.

Once the recruitment of artists has been set into motion, selection of the show site must be finalized. Because of unpredictable weather conditions, which can result in considerable headaches for the promoter, the popular seasonal outdoor events have obvious drawbacks. Preferred are suitable indoor spaces that receive heavy traffic, such as shopping malls, lobbies of large office buildings and hotels, convention facilities, and any meeting place for large group gatherings. Other desirable locations are lobbies of large corporations and banks, and the foyer of the local civic auditorium. Finally, don't overlook the opportunity of making an art show the highpoint of a fund-raising drive for local schools or other institutions.

Advertising in your daily newspaper and in the weekly community paper is an effective way of attracting visitors to an upcoming art show. By all means, see if you can interest a newspaper in publishing an interview with you, the show promoter, or a feature article

about the forthcoming show. Inexpensive signs and banners and a colorful handbill can also be effective publicity tools.

Examine as many art shows as you can before going into business. Also investigate your community's license, liability, and sales tax requirements. An established local attorney, accountant, and insurance professional can aid you in complying with service-related regulations. Remember to start your first venture with simple financial arrangements, and to increase your investment in exhibitions only after you have become experienced in negotiating with exhibitors and proprietors of exhibition sites.

Suggested Reading

Long, Steve, and Cindy Long. *You Can Make Money from Your Arts and Crafts*. Scotts Valley, Calif.: Mark Publications, 1988.

56

Seminar Promotion: The Profitable Marketing of Knowledge

Are you skilled and experienced in the areas of public speaking, negotiating, adult education, research, or agency management? Do you live in or near a bustling metropolitan area? If your answers are yes, the promotion of seminars, a fascinating new career, could be for you.

You have the choice of becoming a *seminar presenter* (well suited for individuals with a good record in public speaking and presentations) or a *manager of independent seminar speakers* (for those with managerial background and an affinity for public relations). The latter activity provides a valuable service to corporations, clubs, public institutions, churches, and other organizations.

Let's take a close look at the key elements of a successful seminar. The lecturers pass along useful information or advice to the audience by means of an oral presentation, supplemented by printed handouts that handily summarize reference material on the subject under discussion. Lively interaction between lecturer and audience is sustained over a period of several hours. Also vital to success are comfortable seating, refreshment breaks, and, of course, an effective promotion to attract a sizable audience. Furthermore, the carefully chosen, appealing topic must match the target group, which can be made up of members of professional, business, or civic organizations, special interest groups, or the general public.

Subjects of general interest—the environmental challenge, coping with the avalanche of new technologies, recognizing hidden business opportunities, overcoming economic adversity, or surviving in an increasingly competitive world—will be timely for years to come. These and similar subjects should draw the general public and issue-related professions and groups to lecture halls.

Metropolitan areas have an abundance of institutions for higher education and adult education, civic clubs, and conventions, all of which are likely to tap the lecturer pool. On the other hand, lecturing to special professional and business groups can be more profitable. Because seminar fees are considered business expenses, they generally exceed those charged to the general public. The minimum fee paid by an attendee at a seminar is $15.

Prospective attendees can be reached through professional and business networks. Take advantage of the seminar previews printed in some business publications; these will provide valuable free advertisements.

Endorsements of future seminars can be secured through organizations, such as medical/health-care networks, the local chamber of commerce, the Small Business Administration, and other professional associations. It is up to you, however, to convince the organization's representative that the seminar package will benefit his/her constituency. A seminar can also become an important part of planned corporate or organizational weekend activities.

Seminars targeted for the general public require considerable more promotional efforts. In addition to newspaper advertisements with possible editorial seminar preview, you may have to generate up to one thousand direct mailings. Depending on the nature of the subject, extend your contacts even to organizations remotely associated with the topic. Ask to have a notice tacked to their bulletin boards and flyers distributed to their members. If available, ask for a free seminar announcement in their internal publications.

If managing seminar presenters appeals to you, the major task is to locate reputable speakers. They can be recruited from all interest areas and all parts of the country. Your main library can assist you in locating accomplished speakers with expert knowledge or qualified authorities, some of whom are also popular book authors. Major public libraries have cataloged the names of a variety of trained speakers. And librarians will gladly help connect you to publishers if you are planning to engage distinguished authors. Celebrated writers turned lecturers have become crowd pleasers at prominent social and fund-raising functions.

Generally, the manager's compensation consists of a percentage of the presenter's fee plus expenses. Because prominent speakers will command handsome fees, the practice is to engage local businesses to underwrite co-sponsored lectures, seminars, or social events.

Regardless of which route you choose, you'll want to contact competent local professionals at the planning stage and examine with their help your community's license, tax, and bonding regulations. Once in business, build up your bookings gradually. If necessary, modify presentation techniques, and remain flexible. Your primary expenditures are the promotional costs, hall rentals, and speaker-related expenses.

Seminar promoting can be an immensely satisfying undertaking, for it offers rare opportunities to meet open-minded people who eagerly wish to broaden their horizons and fascinating speakers with an acute desire to share their expertise.

Suggested Reading

Erbe, Jack. *How to Make Money Running Your Own Weekend Workshops*. Van Nuys, Calif.: Publishers' Services, 1981.

Materka, Pat R. *Workshops and Seminars: Planning, Promoting, Producing Profiting*. Englewood Cliffs, N.J.: Prentice-Hall, 1986.

Murray, Sheila L. *How to Organize and Manage a Seminar*. Englewood Cliffs, N.J.: Prentice-Hall, 1983.

Ruhe-Schoen, Janet. *Organizing and Operating Profitable Workshop Classes*. Babylon, N.Y.: Pilot Books, 1980. (Order from Pilot Books, 103 Cooper Street, Babylon, NY 11702.)

57

Proofreading Is a Service in Demand

Remember when you were an eager participant in your school's spelling competition? Perhaps English spelling and grammar remained areas of special interest in your life. You might even have put them to use professionally, as an English teacher, librarian, or tutor. If so, consider becoming a free-lance proofreader.

Have today's advanced typewriters and word processors with their memory spelling feature reduced the need for proofreading? By no means! Although the average American office may show signs of improved spelling, the need for scrutinizing all facets of any text going into print is greater than ever.

To establish yourself as a self-employed proofreader could be a challenging and satisfying way to capitalize on your knowledge and past experience. Proofreading is frequently interpreted too narrowly. It requires more than just being knowledgeable in orthography. The proofreader must be able to correct English spelling, punctuation, and sentence structure, in addition to sometimes checking presented figures, proper names, facts.

If necessary, strengthen your knowledge of English grammar by taking some advanced courses at your community college. Or you may decide on home studies with the assistance of up-to-date textbooks and audio cassettes.

The list of professions and businesses, as well as organizations and institutions, in need of outside proofreading assistance is extensive. Remember, this is the printed information age, and everyone with something to say wants to be heard. First there are the commercial printers from the smallest to the largest. They are closely followed by the publishers of news communications, specialty printers (of directories, catalogs, business forms), manufacturers, businesses, large health institutions—many of which maintain their own in-house printing departments. Further, there are the large retail establishments with extensive printing needs, typing and secretarial services, advertising and public relations agencies.

Generally, newspapers and magazine publishers, book publishers, and other large establishments in the printing field maintain professional proofreaders on their staff. The exceptions are those businesses that have streamlined their office staff and, therefore, rely on outside free-lance proofreaders.

Frequently, proofreading fees are based upon a per-printed-page charge. Since payment methods vary from one region to another, research the fees that local businesses, including typing and secretarial services, will pay for this service.

As a low-investment activity, a proofreading service can be operated from a small home office. Reliable typing equipment for your communication needs and a telephone answering machine, together with office supplies and a set of up-to-date reference books, will be sufficient to get you started. Don't forget to investigate your community's license, tax, and bonding regulations that pertain to free-lancers.

To spread the word about your new venture, have a quick printing service assist you in designing an attractive circular. Together with a cover letter and business card, distribute the material to area businesses, professional offices, and agencies as specified above. Contact the individual in charge of the organization's communication and/or printing department and, if necessary, follow up with telephone calls; make sure you can supply names of references upon request. Also introduce yourself to local writers' and manuscripts' clubs. And finally, to make your service known to the general public, place some classified ads in local daily newspapers and business publications.

58

||||➡ ⬅||||

Résumé Service: More than Just Accurate Typing

What do former executives and employees from the corporate personnel world, employment agencies, or the career training field have in common? All will qualify for, and will likely be interested in, this appealing, action-filled opportunity to establish a new independent service career: résumé writing. During the past decade, résumé counseling and writing, as well as the typesetting, printing, and duplication of résumés, have become more sophisticated. The growth potential of this unique service is everywhere evident.

But where can you find people in need of a résumé service? You can easily locate them in both small and large communities, in both good times and times of economic downturn. One group seeking assistance includes recent graduates of colleges, vocational institutions, commercial and trade schools. In addition to these first-job applicants, there are those entering the job market after a longer absence, those seeking to change jobs to advance their career, and those looking for work after being laid off.

Applicants for middle- and upper-management and technical positions, who originally were the primary group using professional résumé services, are today only one among many types of job seekers utilizing these services. In fact, in most areas, the majority of job seekers look for professional assistance with their résumés. To familiarize yourself with the sheer volume and variety of prospective clients, just scan the "Help Wanted" and "Job Wanted" sections of your local newspaper(s).

Let me briefly review the kind of services now being offered to those seeking employment. Enterprising résumé service owners have gone from furnishing custom-tailored typewritten résumés to supplying elaborate typesetting and printing services. Others have established résumé counseling and image services for their clients; some even provide assistance with the job search. And then there are communication businesses that offer complete electronic printing service with electronic storage and updating, and, if desired, mass mailings. Others furnish not only résumés but also cover and follow-up letters, along with query letters designed to motivate a business or company to request an interview with the applicant.

Composing effective résumés is no well-kept secret. There are a variety of comprehensive books available at your public library; some aim at special professional groups. They are filled with instructions and samples that show how to formulate attention-getting résumés.

Résumé fees vary according to the service provided. Investigate the pricing in your area. Most fees are based on an hourly rate charged for consultation, composing, and duplication. It is customary, however, to request from the client a money deposit at the time you accept the client's business.

Because you will need access to a reliable duplication service, you may want to contact a number of local copy shops and quick printers before selecting the one you want to work with. It is in your and the establishment's interest to work out a mutually beneficial agreement that will give you a percentage of the business you pass along. Printing and duplicating establishments are also good sources for locating your own prospective clients. Ask the proprietors to display your business card or circular. Your service will complement their own business lines.

Your promotional efforts should begin with some classified newspaper advertisements. These ads should be conspicuously placed so as to be noticed by the numerous job hunters who scan the employment section each day. Then visit various local educational institutions, including colleges that maintain their own employment service, and advertise in their newsletters and bulletins. Also make your activity known among educational job counselors, as well as local employment agencies. All of them can direct clients your way, even if the competition has beaten you to the door. There is always room for a second or third résumé service.

Watch for announcements of business layoffs or closings in your community, and communicate without delay with the personnel managers of such establishments. Since most employers are anxious to assist their soon-to-be-laid-off workers, they may hire you to teach effective résumé writing if you can formulate an appealing program.

Examine your area's license, liability, and tax laws before setting up your new venture. Be sure to seek counseling from established local professionals.

Suggested Reading

Krannich, Ronald L., and William J. Bannis. *High Impact Resumes and Letters*, 4th ed. Manassas, Va.: Impact Publications, 1990.

Parker, Yana. *The Damn Good Resume Guide*. Berkeley, Calif.: Ten Speed Press, 1986.

Washington, Tom. *Resume Power*. Bellevue, Wash.: Mt. Vernon Press, 1985.

59

Beginning Writers: Take Advantage of a Vast Market

Have you procrastinated until now? The time has come for anyone with acknowledged or untested writing ability to finally make his or her long-standing dream come true! Explore the following opportunities, for at no time have they been more plentiful.

Be realistic and expect only modest earnings in the beginning. Start by drafting your own well-constructed blueprint with clear-cut objectives one and two years hence. This will allow you to gradually broaden the scope of your writing, thus increasing the chance for a more substantial steady income.

First, let's focus on the often overlooked *short articles* and *filler-type features* which offer splendid opportunities for new writers to enter the market and ease into the field at their own pace. This activity can become the springboard for more challenging writing ventures (for example, the sizzling how-to publication market, discussed in Chapter 61). A short article consists of at least two paragraphs, and the filler variety ranges from fifty to one thousand words.

Fillers run the gamut from anecdotes, short humor, jokes, to gags, facts, newsbreaks. Leafing through the volumes of consumer magazines in your public library will make you aware of the extensive use of filler material. Trade, technical, and professional magazines utilize fillers as well, occasionally slanted to specific subjects. Who is supplying those fillers? The publishing industry purchases a substantial amount from free-lance writing sources.

You can become a member of this filler-supply network. Each publication has its own targeted readership, style, and requirements. It's easy enough to study them and comply with the specifications. But what should you write about? First of all, recognize your own forte. That is, take stock of your special interests and the wealth of your life experiences, both personal and professional. Your own background can become the source of a consistent stream of ideas. For example, are you an efficient homemaker? Then household cleaning tips, sewing advice, child-care hints, among others, can evolve as natural subjects. Animal lovers can write about pet care and behavior. The person who tinkers in the basement workshop can summarize household and tool repair tips. The experienced gardener has plenty to write about indoor and outdoor plant concepts and care. An abundance of writing ideas should come easily to the seasoned traveler, educator, health-care or law professional, hobbyist, decorator, tradesperson, experienced cook, aviator, hunter, or water sporter, just to name a few.

Even those with a flair for *letter writing* can sell their creative products to a number of American publications. If you are adept at writing letters and enjoy the challenge of creating colorful and absorbing compositions, examine the requirements of various confession-type magazines. These publications buy a great deal of free-lance letter material.

Once you have discovered your writing preferences, head for your nearest public library. Look up the two most important where-and-how-to-sell information sources every serious, published writer consults: the current *Writer's Market* and *The Writer's Handbook*. These publications will provide all necessary specifications, selling and rate information. They will also assist you in shaping and polishing your writings into publishable and marketable manuscripts.

Another way of practicing creative writing is to compose *greeting card verse*. Although it is a competitive field, the greeting card industry does buy material from original and talented free-lance writers. If you have a knack for specialized two-, four-, or six-liners, the industry requirements will be well worth exploring.

Or would you like to apply your creative talent to the field of *puzzles*? If you master puzzle designing, by all means, you should look into what this evolving market has to offer. Imagine, receiving checks for designing puzzles, which are fun to work on from beginning to end!

As you progress in your writing venture, you will need legal counseling. Select a local attorney specializing in publication law.

Suggested Reading

Grenier, Mildred B. *The Beginner's Guide to Writing for a Profit*. Babylon, N.Y.: Pilot Books, 1987. (Order from Pilot Books, 103 Cooper Street, Babylon, NY 11702.)

Jerome, Judson. *The Poet's Handbook*. Cincinnati: Writer's Digest Books, 1980.

McLarn, Jack Clinton. *Writing Part-Time for Fun and Money*. Wilmington: Enterprise Publishers, 1984. (Covers business, confessions, and script writing, and children's articles. Order from Enterprise Publishing, Inc., 725 N. Market Street, Wilmington, DE 19801.)

Neff, Glenda Tennant, ed. *Writer's Market*. Cincinnati: Writer's Digest Books, 1991.

Raskin, Julie, and Carolyn Males. *How to Write and Sell a Column*. Cincinnati: Writer's Digest Books, 1987.

Zinsser, William. *On Writing Well: An Informal Guide to Writing Nonfiction*. 3d ed. New York: Harper and Row, 1985.

60

Part-time Reporter, Chronicler: Make Local News Your Business

Wouldn't you love to see your news reports in print every week? For a stimulating part-time writing career, become a *free-lance reporter*. Tested writing skills, flexibility, resourcefulness, and a knack for easily mixing and conversing with people are essential qualities for success in the field.

To augment and update your journalistic training, take extension courses or college-level continuing-education classes. Or investigate the courses offered by reputable writing schools if you lack confidence in your current writing skills and in how-to-sell-what-you-write. The nonfiction-writing correspondence courses are an excellent preparation for professional writing. Because these courses teach students how to write material that meets today's professional standards and is highly marketable, they are well worth the tuition investment. As an added bonus, students of all ages can earn money by selling their writing assignments while progressing in their studies. If uncertain about selecting a reputable writing school, contact the *Writer's Digest* magazine, 1507 Dana Avenue, Cincinnati, OH 45207; (800) 289-0963.

As a free-lance writer, you will need to find legal counseling. Select a reputable attorney well versed in the publication field before going into business.

Because of the great diversity of community life, you'll find much that is worth reporting. Concentrate on any area you are comfortable with: business, social, or educational reporting. (It's best to leave political reporting to those on newspaper staffs.) Let's begin with business reporting, including coverage of company/store openings, anniversaries, personnel promotions, business expansions and moves to new buildings, export publicity, import showcase events, trade shows, new products, government-sponsored workshops, local inventions, retail mall events, seasonal commercial fairs, and arts and crafts shows.

The social sector covers a wide range of activities as well. Worth reporting is news pertaining to local clubs and other organizations: details of meetings, installations of new officers and board members, galas and parties, award ceremonies, and charity affairs. Also newsworthy are community projects, new citizens and their new-life stories, welcoming and farewell of the clergy, institutional and church bazaars, civic fundraising projects, ethnic groups' happenings. And don't overlook anniversaries and transitions of well-known citizens, their legacy and impact on the community.

The educational field is equally extensive. You can report on the full range of local school and sports events, unique programs or summer activities, student awards, higher education workshops, and minority education.

Finally, there is the weekly reporting on outings within your hometown and to surrounding areas. A one-day excursion can include visits to neighboring counties or to seasonal cultural events. Report on theme parks, restaurants, inns and markets, on fairs, campgrounds, outdoor theater productions, and sports events, all within a day's drive from home.

Or what about the *chronicling*? Regional historic places, buildings, museums, monuments, churches, parks, cemeteries, neighborhoods, and regional cultural events are plentiful everywhere. They all are waiting to be rediscovered.

With some shining samples of your published or unpublished news reports or chronicles, make contact with your area's publishers of newspapers or weekly neighborhood and trade papers. Skip the large corporate publishers, and concentrate on medium-sized and small firms which favor the use of free-lance reporters or chroniclers to complement their staff. Free-lance reporting plays a particularly important role at publishing houses where cutbacks of full-time staff reporters are evident.

The news business is highly competitive, so don't lose heart if you encounter snarls along the way. Your perseverance and earnest diligent writing efforts will be richly rewarded in the end. The fascinating contacts, the entrée to organizations and institutions, the recognition within your community, plus the financial compensation—all will uniquely enrich your life.

Suggested Reading

Hensley, Dennis E., and Holly G. Miller. *The Freelance Writer's Handbook*. New York: Harper and Row, 1987.

Murray, Donald. *Writing for Your Readers*. Chester, Conn.: Globe Pequot Press, 1981.

Whitmeyer, Claude; Salli Rasberry; and Michael Phillips. *Running a One-Person Business*. Berkely, Calif.: Ten Speed Press, 1989.

© Polly Keener 1991

61

||||▶ ◀||||

Write How-to Books or
Sell Information
via Mail Order

Admit it! Haven't you entertained the notion of authoring a best-selling how-to book or information report? The public's appetite for such material appears to be insatiable. Information sales opportunities have surpassed experts' predictions, and the demand is expected to continue unabated into the twenty-first century.

How can someone with, or without, proven writing ability jump on this fast-moving bandwagon of *how-to-books and articles*? He or she must select a subject with broad appeal and be able to skillfully communicate an expert knowledge of this subject to the reading public. Round off the requirements with common sense, some negotiation ability, diligence, and perseverance.

The scope of subjects to write about is limitless. A glance at the shelves of bookstores and libraries will convince you. It seems that everything from "How to Collect Abacuses" to "How to Get the Most Out of Properly Prepared Zucchini" is waiting for buyers or readers. Popular subjects explored in print include family dynamics, daily living, food, home care, education, sports, travel, health care, pets, entertainment. Here are some imaginary examples: from the lofty "How to Survive Near the Top of the Management Ladder with

Three Belly Laughs a Day" to the feet-on-the-ground "How to Turn Your Onion Harvest into Prize-Winning Party Food," from the neighborly "How to Raise a Pit Bull and Still Remain a Popular Neighbor" to the pragmatic "How to Live on Half of Your Retirement Income While Merrily Traveling on the Other."

Whether you intend to write a book or an article, your first step should be to consult the current eight-volume set of *Books in Print* at your public library. This reference indexes publications by author's name, book title, and subject. If you can't find the subject you want to write about among the entries in *Books in Print*, consider yourself lucky. More likely, you'll discover a publication that deals with some aspect of the subject matter. Yet your own thorough knowledge of the topic, supported by intensive research (take advantage of all public libraries in your area), can make you uniquely qualified to give the material a new slant.

You have nothing to lose, but everything to gain, by first plunging into writing and marketing a few how-to articles. This will strengthen your knowledge of the subject and teach you the ins and outs of the market, both of which can be applied to your more laborious efforts on a booklet or full-size publication.

If your writing skills need some fine-tuning, attend community college classes, lectures, seminars, even writers' conferences. Also familiarize yourself with effective interview techniques, for you need to query experts in the chosen field.

Mail-order information selling is a related opportunity for free-lance writers. Do you thrive on challenge? Are you a planner and doer and also blessed with business savvy? Then writing and selling information via mail order can be the direct route to a very prosperous life-style, as a number of well-publicized success stories confirm. According to the U.S. Department of Commerce, in its publication *Establishing and Operating a Mail Order Business*: "Mail order operators who specialize in selling bits of education can produce very profitable and satisfactory results. Further, it is an easy way to get started and is one of the most profitable areas of mail order selling."

You can sell information on any subject you are confident with and which, in your judgment, will appeal to a large segment of the public. You may try your hand at somewhat more conservative subjects than those listed earlier in the chapter. What about "How to Turn an Ordinary Side-Dish Salad into a Delicious Gourmet Meal" or "Little-Known Facts on How to Travel in Style and Get Paid for It"?

Here is how the process works. Let's say you have uncovered a commonsense way to inexpensively, safely, and successfully rid your garden of ordinary pests. In plain English, commit your discovery to one or two sheets of paper and add a title sheet that also displays your copyright symbol. (The current copyright procedure, simple and inexpensive, is discussed in specialty library books.) Then reproduce your typewritten pages, staple them, fold them, so that one set will easily fit into a number-10 envelope. In cases where the mail-order information is extensive, it may have to be put on as many as fifty to a hundred pages, bound in a soft cover. Of course, producing a publication of this size requires the services of an efficient, reasonable printer and possibly a graphic designer.

Mail-order publications are sold directly to the consumer, with prices starting at $3 plus a stamped, self-addressed envelope for a two-page report to $15 (handling included) for a comprehensive softcover.

To maximize earnings, and minimize expenses, mail-order sellers place classified ads with one or several of the dozens of national magazines that target the readers they want to reach. The capsule (up to twenty-five-word) ads are dressed up with catchy headings to draw maximum attention to cleverly titled publications. Though slow in the beginning, the selling pace will pick up once you gain experience in the advertising area. You can also expand your promotional efforts to direct mailings. This, however, requires some trade know-how, for you must purchase the best-suited mailing lists from a wide range of sources.

Even well-regarded specialty *subscription newsletters* have been launched at the start-from-scratch, part-time level. But unlike information selling, such a venture requires a larger financial commitment, years of hard work, and a team of dedicated family members.

Any of the profiled writing services require counsel by competent local professionals. For other aspects of the mail-order business, see Chapter 51.

Suggested Reading

Biagi, Shirley. *Interviews That Work*. Belmont, Calif.: Wadsworth, 1986.

Books in Print, 1990-91. 8 vols. New York: Bowker, 1990.

Hull, Raymond. *How to Write How-to Books and Articles*. Cincinnati: Writer's Digest Books, 1984.

Riddle, John. *Writing and Selling Information the Mail Order Way*. Babylon, N.Y.: Pilot Books, 1985. (Order from Pilot Books, 103 Cooper Street, Babylon, NY 11702.)

Small Business Administration. *Selling by Mail Order*. (See Appendix B for details on how to order this pamphlet.)

62

Want to Work with a Travel Agency? Attractive Benefits for Those Who Qualify

So you are enthusiastic about traveling—crossing this continent, hopping to foreign countries, and cruising near and far oceans. But can you convey your enthusiasm to a demanding clientele? And what about your ability to handle the tedious technical aspects of the travel business? You must be an experienced traveler who possesses good communication skills; a well-organized, meticulous, and detail-oriented individual; and in good physical condition to qualify for the stimulating and financially rewarding opportunities in the travel field.

According to industry analysts, this field is expected to expand over the next ten years. The projected industry growth, as well as the sporadic departure of experienced agents from the profession, will ensure a steady flow of openings in the travel business. But take note:

it's a competitive and hectic business, particularly if you share in the responsibilities of travel preparations!

Peter D'Attoma, president of DaVinci Travel Group, Inc., emphasizes the importance of patience, tactfulness, and the ability to withstand stress and work pressure. He points out that travel agency personnel are positioned in the frontline of this multifaceted industry. And the work pace can become hectic during peak travel seasons. Also highly valued is sales ability coupled with credibility, which entails gaining the confidence of the client and giving out information in a knowledgeable, factual manner. After all, the objectives of any successful service business are customer satisfaction and cultivation of the clientele's repeat business.

Opportunities to become affiliated with the travel business depend largely on the applicant's qualifications, availability of time, as well as size and location of the travel agency. Although in the past it was common practice for agency personnel to start their careers with on-the-job training, today's applicants will find that employers prefer to hire those with a college degree or specialized schooling. Some travel agencies would rather hire exclusively full-time, salaried *agents*, while others have openings for self-employed part-time *travel consultants* or *counselors*. People of all age groups have been hired as employees, as well as self-employed associates.

The larger the community and the more travel agencies it supports, the broader the choices for applicants. The *Occupational Outlook Handbook, 1988/89* reports that about 40 percent of all travel agencies are in large cities; about 47 percent in suburban areas; and only about 10 percent in small towns and rural areas.

Employed agency personnel, consultants, and counselors routinely handle arrangements of transportation, hotel accommodations, tours, vacation packages. They also furnish information on fares, schedules, packaged tours, and cruises. While they must know the products they sell, self-employed consultants spend time outside the office, as well, to generate new business. Building up a client following is an important sales function.

A special type of sales consultant hired by travel agencies is the *independent contractor*, sometimes also called an *account executive*. He or she is primarily active in metropolitan areas with their diverse blend of industry, business, civic organizations, and educational institutions. A well-informed professional familiar with all phases of the travel business, the independent contractor is expected to utilize his or her sales ability to build up a stable business following among corporate and business travelers. Cultivation of group travel, travel incentives, and travel clubs are an essential part of the professional's activities.

Self-employed agency associates are occasionally called upon to make slide or video presentations to special interest groups and social clubs. And their participation at area trade shows and exhibitions is not uncommon.

A relatively new staff addition at sizable travel agencies serving foreign tourist groups is the *bi-* or *multilingual travel consultant*. With the influx of foreign tourists into this country, the number of travel consultants who escort groups of foreign visitors to certain regions is on the rise.

The wage levels for travel business employees are determined by experience, sales ability, size, and location of the establishment. Self-employed consultants and independent contractors with superior sales skills, whose compensation is primarily derived from commission earnings, can raise their income above the level of salaried agency personnel. However, it's rarely done without diligent work efforts. The travel agencies' commission earnings from airlines are between 8 and 10 percent, while other travel suppliers and tour operators generally pay 10 to 15 percent, according to the American Society of Travel Agents (ASTA).

And what about the sought-after travel discounts for the personnel? With some exceptions and after a certain probation period, self-employed associates, like agency employees, will also become eligible for travel discounts of varying degrees. An added bonus will be the eligibility for FAM trips (familiarization trips). Costs for these promotional tours are partially shared by airlines, resort and hotel concerns, as well as cruiseship companies. Participation rules, as well as reimbursement of trip expenses, are not uniformly enforced within the travel business.

If you are serious about joining this industry, update your current knowledge by signing up for travel courses at your community college or continuing-education institution. Or take a course at one of the accredited commercial travel schools that operate in many cities. Since agency work is largely computerized, be sure to familiarize yourself with computer operations.

You can write to the American Society of Travel Agents, P.O. Box 23992, Washington, DC 20026, for informative literature and listings of travel schools.

Suggested Reading

Stevens, Lawrence. *Your Career in Travel and Tourism.*
Wheaton, Ill.: Merton House, 1981. (Order from
Merton House Publishing Co., 937 West Liber-
ty Drive, Wheaton, IL 60187.)

63

Bus Tours Are Fun: Become a Group Tour Coordinator

Niagara Falls, Santa Fe, Lake Tahoe, or Disney
World—wouldn't you like to travel in a comfortable,
climate-controlled motorcoach several times a month to
memorable locations everyone is talking about? Coordinating bus tours not only guarantees you a free seat on
the tour you organize, but rewards your work with a lucrative commission.

Presently, for millions of citizens throughout the
country, one-day and multiday bus touring has become
an enormously popular leisure time pursuit. To cash in
on the boom, touring companies are expanding their
services to smaller communities by setting up a far-
reaching agent network. And that means more openings
for those interested in working for the multifaceted
tourist business.

An increasing number of individuals have been taking advantage of opportunities to become *group tour*

coordinators, also called *organizers*, or *agents*. Although self-employed and operating independently, they are affiliated with motorcoach touring companies frequently headquartered in a location different from the coordinator's residence. Such a service is particularly suited for couples or friends that work well together as a team. To qualify, candidates must be people-oriented and willing to work odd hours. Likewise, they must be trustworthy, possess organizational talent, and be imaginative and capable of coping with emergency situations.

Depending on the business generated, a group tour coordinator's commission can add up to handsome earnings. Monetary compensation, benefits, and responsibilities are subject to variations within the touring industry. It's left to the coordinator's discretion whether or not to escort a client's bus tour. Sometimes coordinators choose to delegate the function to a trained family member or friend.

How large is the average touring group? And are the buses easy to fill? Generally, one-day tour rates are based on thirty-eight passengers and up, multiday-tour rates on thirty-eight to forty-four passengers. Most companies charge a fixed sum for optional escort service. As a rule, the coordinator is given the option of offering one or two free seats to the client group. Sometimes such a windfall for the client is used to benefit the group's fund-raising.

With the bulk of the tour arrangements handled by the touring company staff, the coordinator's prime function is to negotiate and discuss with group representatives everything from tour planning and customizing to rates and savings. Moreover, the coordinator collects fare deposits and final group payments. The well-informed coordinator also is on hand with suggestions about entertainment, selection of eating places, meals, little-known sightseeing spots, and discount sales outlets. Frequently, he or she is called upon to offer ideas to make the tour exciting and fun, as well as to make tour presentations at committee meetings and group gatherings.

What kind of people are interested in taking bus excursions? A group tour coordinator cultivates clients among a variety of groups. Senior living centers and retirement communities are generally the first to be approached. Other prospects are church groups, members of art museums (to visit major cities and art exhibitions), social clubs, and commercial enterprises. When contacting the business firms, suggest that they treat their employees to annual mystery bus tours, visits to the state fair or to a big-city dinner theater, trips to lectures or sports events.

While maintaining an up-to-date mailing list, at the beginning of the touring season the coordinator mails a composite tour listing to client groups, including commercial prospects. At the beginning of the spring and fall travel seasons, he or she also utilizes local media advertising. All promotional expenses are part of the coordinator's operating budget.

Vera Lowe is an excellent example of how enterprising persons can turn a new entrepreneurial challenge into an enjoyable, fulfilling, and profitable service. This cheerful, gracious, and dedicated woman successfully operates a group tour service in the Midwest. And her following keeps growing. Her secret? Treat each traveler with respect, and provide thoughtful, personalized service at affordable rates.

Anyone interested in working in the fascinating touring industry should contact several local touring companies and inquire about their agent network. Most companies will assist their agents with the administrative aspects of the business. If you plan to operate a service as an independent agent, first seek counsel from reputable local professionals (attorney, accountant, insurance professional) on complying with your area's business requirements.

Suggested Reading

Boe, Beverly, and Phil Philcox. *How You Can Travel Free as a Group Tour Organizer.* Babylon, N.Y.: Pilot Books, 1987. (Order from Pilot Books, 103 Cooper Street, Babylon, NY 11702.)

64

The Fascinating World of International Touring

This month it could be a transatlantic flight to Spain with ensuing Mediterranean cruise. Next month the travel schedule may call for the tour escort to take a touring group on a combination air-cruise journey to

Alaska. Sound exciting? Of course—it will delight any globe-trotter. Both younger and mature individuals have taken advantage of a variety of business opportunities for free worldwide touring. In some instances, it's free air travel; in others, all accommodations paid plus commission; in still others, a paycheck may be awaiting upon the traveler's return.

Who are these fortunate travel enthusiasts, and what background and qualifications are required to become successful in this competitive business? Among the successful, I discovered dynamic persons in their thirties, as well as a surprising number of vigorous early retirees and senior citizens. Their professional background? A large percentage had at one time been educators, librarians, researchers, administrators, and members of the travel industry. What do they have in common? Foremost, extensive international travel experience. They are also self-starters, good organizers; they have enthusiasm as well as patience. Many work in a team of two or more, be it spouse, family member, or friend.

Let's first focus on the *touring coordinator* or *tour organizer*. This individual will cultivate a group of people seriously interested in participating in a packaged overseas trip for a special purpose. The tour coordinator's efforts can develop into a tour to the Scandinavian countries to trace the participants' ancestral roots, or to Central Europe to visit famous performing arts festivals, or to an international professional convention in Singapore. After the group is collected, the next step is to find the best possible deal on an all-inclusive package from a travel agent or tour supplier. Contact a number of businesses, all of which will welcome the opportunity to bid on your tour. Once you make your selection, the chosen firm will handle all the touring arrangements and will offer you a free slot in exchange for a group of at least ten paying travelers. Most likely, you will attract a larger group and, depending on several additional factors, you will be eligible for a second free trip ticket. What a splendid opportunity for a travel-oriented couple to earn a transportation-paid trip to Alaska, Mexico, Africa, or even the Orient.

The loosely used title *tour director* is sometimes bestowed on single individuals or couples who work closely with national professional associations and their retired membership. These associations regularly sponsor packaged worldwide tours which are managed by national tour suppliers. Tour directors escort such touring groups and furnish the sponsoring organization with a travel report upon completion of each tour. Most tour directors have years of extensive international travel experience to their credit and, occasionally, are bilingual. Many of them receive not only complimentary travel and hotel accommodations, but also a financial reward (based on daily or weekly rates) for their often strenuous efforts to ensure a smoothly run journey. Tour directors are frequently supported at foreign destinations by native travel guides who, in turn, are the link to the foreign tour promoter.

During the peak of the travel season, providers frequently release several touring groups within short intervals to the same foreign destination. Circumstances like this make it necessary for the tour director to remain, at times, for several weeks at a particular foreign hub to receive and direct the arriving groups.

Matching perfectly the description of experienced tour directors are the retired couple Glen and Grace

Mayes. Residing in the Midwest, they have shared their
globe-trotting expertise with countless satisfied American tourists and, over the years, have built up an enthusiastic and loyal following. During the travel season,
their life can become fast-paced, for occasional back-to-
back foreign touring can make trying demands on anyone's energy. Working as a team, this charming and
tireless couple share the wealth of their touring experience with future professionals at evening classes of the
local continuing-education institution.

Another way to launch a free-lance career in international group touring is to become a *tour operator*. For
example, if you have a preference for, or an affiliation
with, a particular foreign location, you can concentrate
on taking American tourist groups to this destination as
many times as you can logistically manage. Even if you
choose to get assistance from professional tour providers, you can incorporate your own individualized travel
ideas into a customized tour package.

Or, if you so desire, you can establish your own state-
licensed and bonded business. As the *owner of a tour
promoting company*, you can offer interest groups
around the country your personally mapped out, specialized international tours. You even have the option of
handling the total travel package, or, for example, turning over the air transportation to a reputable travel agent
or airline. Be aware, however, that a computerized tour
operator business involves a myriad of details and pre-
suppose business savvy, a healthy appetite for challenges, and competent associates.

President of his own Alpine tour company, Cecil
Dobbins, another energetic and enterprising midwest-
erner, together with his family, is the perfect example of

how to successfully break into the prolific specialized touring market. As many as eight times a year, Cecil takes groups of up to twelve travelers to the "hikers paradise," the trails of the Swiss Alps. His individualized, soft-adventure style of Alpine touring has sparked interest among mountain hikers around the country.

What should you do to create interest in your own tours? With the preliminary tour itinerary in hand and by means of well-prepared slide or video presentations, you can generate interest among members of civic and sports clubs, churches, educational institutions, and professional associations. Other groups to be approached are senior citizens' communities and organizations, social and ethnic clubs. Specialized tour promotion may require placing advertisements in regional and national magazines or association and trade papers, far in advance of the touring seasons. By all means, get yourself booked for the travel series slide presentations at public library branches. These travelogues are usually well publicized in the local press. It will surprise you how easily you can round up prospects for future tours.

Finally, a few words about the professional *tour manager*, who is primarily affiliated with large national tour suppliers. This professional is expected to have several years of experience in tour operating, tour management, and international travel. Considered the representative of the tour supplier, the hotelier, and airline, he or she is hired to ensure the smoothness of group travel. If you are interested in becoming a tour manager, request informative literature from the International Association of Tour Managers, Box 4001, New York, NY 10185.

Unless you become an employee of a travel provider, your independent activities in the travel industry require strict adherence to existing state and municipal regulations. It is imperative to engage the services of competent professionals (attorney, accountant, insurance professional) when organizing your service business.

Suggested Reading

Boe, Beverly, and Phil Philcox. *How You Can Travel Free as a Group Tour Organizer*. Babylon, N.Y.: Pilot Books, 1987. (Includes useful listings of group tour operators, government tourist information offices, and other relevant information. Order from Pilot Books, 103 Cooper Street, Babylon, NY 11702.)

65

⫸ ⫷

More Areas of Expertise, Talents, and Hobbies That Can Be Turned into Thriving Home-based Services

- Addressing and mailing service:

  serving small and retail businesses with heavy mailings

- Car pool coordinator:

  serving local employers

- Coordinating vacation homes for pets:

  serving vacationing pet owners by matching them with compatible pet owners willing to take in an additional pet for the duration of the vacation

- Escort service for the elderly:

  serving individual elderly persons, social clubs, entertainment enterprises

- Floral arranger:

  serving professional offices, restaurants, churches, at-home parties

- Fund-raising consultant:

  to institutions, civic organizations, churches

237

- Making potpourri and fragrant concoctions: selling to gift shops, boutiques, holiday bazaars

- Needlecraft teacher: holding classes at handicraft stores and for private clientele

- Raising small animals for profit: supplying pet shops and pet show owners

- Safety and security consultant: to corporations and businesses; this field is successfully pursued by retired law officers

- Tourist home operator: offering to tourists bed-and-breakfast rooms

- Toxicology consultant: to businesses, hospitals, laboratories, and educational institutions on hazardous waste management

- Travel companion service: offering club membership to single globe-trotters preferring compatible companionship; also working with touring industry

Appendix A

Helpful Organizations

The following governmental agencies were established to assist the small business community:

The *U.S. Small Business Administration (SBA)*, an independent federal agency, provides training and educational programs, advisory services, financial programs, and contract assistance. The agency's emphasis is on advancing owners' managerial skills through workshops, seminars, and conferences. It also offers specialized programs for home-based women and minority entrepreneurs. The SBA makes available an abundance of free or low-cost pamphlets on a wide variety of subjects (for publication information, see Appendix B). SBA offices are located in most major cities. They are listed under U.S. government in the telephone directory. For those wishing "to start their own successful small business," the agency recommends calling (800) 827-5722 (in Washington DC only: 653-7561).

Service Corps of Retired Executives (SCORE), with 13,000 retired and active executives in 400 chapters, is the counseling and training arm of the SBA. SCORE offers free one-on-one counseling and low-cost workshops and training sessions in over 750 locations throughout the country.

Small Business Development Centers (SBDCs) are supported through either federal, state, or local funding. The number of centers is growing. They have spread to many cities where they provide managerial, technical, specialized assistance, as well as networking opportunities. These centers' proliferating Community Enterprises Committees offer valuable service to local women trying to achieve economic self-sufficiency.

The local *Chamber of Commerce*, or *Board of Trade*, or *Regional Development Board* and the municipal *Office of Economic Development* assist would-be entrepreneurs with information on business-related issues; they also foster contacts within the business community.

A carefully chosen local *bank* can develop into an important contact for any home-based businessperson. Therefore, select a bank with a proven service record to small business. Such service goes beyond routine financial transactions and may include counseling on financial matters, furnishing business references, or recommending local professionals vital to any small business operation.

A variety of fields are represented by the following trade and professional organizations:

American Collectors Association, Inc., P.O. Box 39106, Minneapolis, MN 55439; (612) 926-6547

American Home Business Association (AHBA), 397 Post Road, Darien, CT 06820; (203) 655-4380. AHBA distributes to its members information on taxes, equipment, and other topics; additionally, it provides counseling, a health insurance plan, buying services, computer programs, and a monthly publication.

American Society of Home Inspectors, 3299 K Street

NW, 7th Floor, Washington, DC 20007; (202) 842-3096.

Cruise Lines International Association (CLIA), 500 Fifth Avenue, Suite 1407, New York, NY 10110; (212) 425-7400.

Direct Marketing Association, 11 West 42nd Street, New York, NY 10036; (212) 768-7277.

Direct Selling Association (DSA), 1776 K Street NW, Suite 600, Washington, DC 20006; (202) 293-5760. Direct your request for a complete listing of active direct-selling companies to this address. The following is a cross section of member companies:

Amer-i-can Fire and Safety Corp., Treavose Manor, 3779 Bristol Road, Bensalem, PA 19020; (215) 750-7373; fire extinguishers

Amway Corporation, 7575 East Fulton Road, Ada, MI 49355; (616) 676-6000; household, personal, home-care products and nutritional supplements

Avacare, Inc., Division of Nutri-Metics International, 19501 East Walnut Drive, City of Industry, CA 91749; (714) 598-1831; cosmetics, hair, and health-care products

Avon Products, Inc., 9 West 57th Street, New York, NY 10019; (212) 546-6015; cosmetics, jewelry

Contempo Fashions, 6100 Broadmoor, Shawnee Mission, KS 66202; (913) 262-7407; jewelry, accessories

The Creative Circle, 15711 South Broadway, Gardena, CA 90248; (213) 327-1931; craft and needlecraft kits

Discovery Toys, Inc. 2530 Arnold Drive, Suite 400, Martinez, CA 94553; (415) 370-7575; educational toys, books, games

Ekco Home Products Company, 2382 Townsgate Road,

Westlake Village, CA 91361; (805) 494-1711; cookware, cutlery

Heart and Home, Inc., P.O. Box 11309, Spring, TX 77391; (713) 320-0266; decorative accessories

The Kirby Company, 1920 West 114th Street, Cleveland, OH 44102; (216) 228-2400; vacuum cleaners

Mary Kay Cosmetics, Inc., 8787 Stemmons Freeway, Dallas, TX 75247; (214) 630-8787; cosmetics

The Pampered Chef, Ltd., P.O. Box 172, River Forest, IL 60305; (312) 366-4059; kitchenware

QW Fashions, 2500 Crawford Avenue, Evanston, IL 60201; (312) 492-1400; women's clothing

Shaklee Corporation, Shaklee Terraces, 444 Market Street, San Francisco, CA 94111; (415) 954-3000; food supplements, foods, personal-care products

Time-Life Books, Inc., 777 Duke Street, Alexandria, VA 22314; (703) 838-7000; educational publications

Tri-Chem, Inc., One Cape May Street, Harrison, NJ 07029; (201) 482-5500; craft products, liquid embroidery paint

Tupperware Home Parties, P.O. Box 2353, Orlando, FL 32802; (407) 847-3111; plastic food storage containers, cookware, children's toys

U.S. Safety & Engineering Corporation, 2365 El Camino Avenue, Sacramento, CA 95821; (916) 482-8888; security systems, fire and burglar alarms

Water Resources International, Inc., 2310 Sherman Street, Phoenix, AZ 85009; (602) 257-0510; water-conditioning and purification systems

World Books, Inc., 510 Merchandise Mart Plaza, Chicago, IL 60654; (312) 245-3456; educational publications

International Association of Tour Managers, Box 4001, New York, NY 10185.

National Association for the Self-Employed (NASE), 2328 Gravel Road, Fort Worth, TX 76118; (817) 589-2475, (800) 232-NASE. In addition to health insurance and retirement plans for the self-employed, NASE offers a newsletter, discounts on business and personal services, and member benefits guide.

National Association of Home Based Businesses (NAHBB), P.O. Box 30220, Baltimore, MD 21270; (301) 363-3698. Promoting the free-enterprise system, NAHBB provides business opportunities, joint mailer service, educational seminars, and information on various topics. It also distributes quarterly publications and semiannual directory.

National Association of Home Inspectors, 5775 Wayzata Boulevard, Minneapolis, MN 55416; (800) 448-3942.

National Federation of Independent Business (NFIB), Suite 700, 600 Maryland Avenue SW, Washington, DC 20024, (202) 554-9000, and 150 W. 20th Avenue, San Mateo, CA 94403, (415) 341-7441. The largest advocacy group for owners of small businesses (over half a million members) lobbies on many issues including taxes, health-care reform, labor, and competition. Its members vote on each issue, and majority vote establishes NFIB position.

Appendix B

||||▶ ◀||||

Useful Business Books, Pamphlets, and Periodicals

The *U.S. Small Business Administration (SBA)*, an independent federal agency, addresses the requirements of new small business owners with a wide range of free and low-cost publications. For a free catalog, or to order any of the pamphlets listed below, write to SBA, P.O. Box 15434, Fort Worth, TX 76119. Make check or money order payable to U.S. Small Business Administration. Prices are subject to change without notice.

The following are only a small selection of the agency's available publications:

Accounting Services for Small Service Firms (FM 6), $0.50

Advertising (MT 11), $1.00

The Business Plan for Home-Based Business (MP 15), $1.00—best-seller

Business Plan for Small Manufacturers (MP 4), $1.00

Evaluating Franchise Opportunities (MP 26), $1.00

Going into Business (MP 12), $0.50—best-seller

How to Get Started with a Small Business Computer (MP 14), $1.00

Ideas into Dollars (PI 1), $2.00

Planning and Goal Setting for Small Business (MP 6), $0.50—best-seller

Pricing Your Products and Services Profitably (FM 13), $1.00

Recordkeeping in a Small Business (FM 10), $1.00—best-seller

Researching Your Market (MT 8), $1.00—best-seller

Selecting the Legal Structure for Your Business (MP 25), $1.00

Selling by Mail Order (MT 9), $1.00

Understanding Cash Flow (FM 4), $1.00

The *Small Business Reporter* series from the Bank of America addresses the needs of new entrepreneurs, small business managers, and their advisers to become and stay successful. The booklets are reasonably priced. Direct catalog request or order to Small Business Reporter, Bank of America, Dept. 3631, P.O. Box 37000, San Francisco, CA 94137. Make check or money order payable to Bank of America. Three selected booklets:

Establishing an Accounting Practice (SBR 119), $5.00

Financial Records for Small Business (SBR 128), $5.00

Steps to Starting a Business (SBR 110), $5.00

Among the great number of books devoted to general business topics, the following titles are especially helpful:

Boyd, Margaret A., compiler. *The Where-to-Sell-It Directory.* Babylon, N.Y.: Pilot Books, 1990.

Cresci, Martha W. *Complete Book of Model Business Letters.* Englewood Cliffs, N.J.: Prentice-Hall, 1986. (281 model letters.)

Goodman, Gary S. *Selling Skills for the Non-Salesperson: For People Who Hate to Sell, But Love to Succeed.* Englewood Cliffs, N.J.: Prentice-Hall, 1984.

Harmon, Charlotte. *The Flea Market Entrepreneur.* Babylon, N.Y.: Pilot Books, 1987.

Husch, Tony, and Linda Foust. *That's a Great Idea, How to Get, Evaluate, Protect, Develop, and Sell New Product Ideas.* Berkeley, Calif.: Ten Speed Press, 1987.

Ingram, Colin. *The Small Business Test.* Berkeley, Calif.: Ten Speed Press, 1990.

Kamoroff, Bernard. *Small Time Operator: How to Start Your Own Business, Keep Your Own Books, Pay Your Taxes and Stay Out of Trouble!* Laytonville, Calif.: Bell Springs, 1990. (Updated annually.)

Krupa, Arlene, with Chris Kirk-Kuwaye. *Couplepower: How to Be Partners in Love and Business.* New York: Dodd, Mead, 1987.

Lant, Jeffrey L. *The Consultant's Kit, Establishing and Operating Your Successful Consulting Business.* 2d ed. Cambridge, Mass.: JLR Publications, 1981.

Silliphant, Leigh, and Sureleigh Silliphant. *Making $70,000-Plus a Year as a Self-Employed Manufacturer's Representative.* Berkeley, Calif.: Ten Speed Press, 1988.

Small, S. T., ed. *1991 Directory of Franchising Organizations.* Babylon, N.Y.: Pilot Books, 1991. (Order from Pilot Books, 103 Cooper Street, Babylon, NY 11702.)

Whitmeyer, Claude; Salli Rasberry; and Michael Phillips. *Running a One-Person Business*. Berkeley, Calif.: Ten Speed Press, 1989.

Wilson, Sandi. *Be the Boss—Start and Run Your Own Service Business*. New York: Avon Books, 1985.

Zuckerman, Laurie. *On Your Own: A Woman's Guide to Building a Business*. Dover, N.H.: Upstart, 1990.

Periodicals for the small business entrepreneur:

Entrepreneur, 2392 Morse Avenue, Irvine, CA 92714. The emphasis is on profitable small business opportunities.

In Business, Box 323, Emmaus, Pa 18409. Published bimonthly, the magazine focuses on environmental entrepreneuring.

Inc., 38 Commercial Wharf, Boston, MA 02110. A magazine for managers of growing small companies ranging from $1 million and up.

Success (Incorporating Success Unlimited), 230 Park Avenue, New York, NY 10169. Calls itself "magazine for the entrepreneurial mind." Stresses importance of entrepreneurial attitude and outlook.

Appendix C

Commonly Used Contract Forms

CONTRACTOR AGREEMENT

Date:

To_____

Address_____

City or Town_____

Dear Sir:

_____propose to furnish all
materials and perform all labor necessary to complete
the following:_____
_____
_____
_____
_____
_____
_____
_____

All of the above work to be completed in a substantial and workmanlike manner according to standard practices or applicable codes for the sum of

_____

_____ Dollars ($_____).

Payments to be made_____

_____

_____

to the value of_____percent (_____%) of all work completed. The entire amount of contract to be paid within _____days after completion.

Any alteration or modification from the above specifications involving extra cost of material or labor will only be executed upon written orders for same, and will become an extra charge over the sum mentioned in this contract. All agreements must be made in writing.

Respectfully submitted,

By:_____

ACCEPTANCE

You are hereby authorized to furnish all materials and labor required to complete the work mentioned in the above proposal, for which_____agree to pay the amount contained in said proposal, and according to the terms thereof.

ACCEPTED   _____

_____

Date_____, 19_____.

CONDITIONAL SALE AGREEMENT

Date:

The undersigned Buyer hereby purchases from

_____

_____

_____ (Seller)
the following goods: (Describe or Attach)

Sales price	$_____
Sales tax (if any)	$_____
Finance charge	$_____
Insurance (if any)	$_____
Other charges (if any)	$_____
Total purchase price	$_____
Less:	
Down payment $_____	
Other credits $_____	
Total credits	$_____
Amount financed	$_____
ANNUAL INTEREST RATE_____%	

The amount financed shall be payable in   (weekly/ monthly) installments of $ each, commencing one (week/month) from date hereof.

Seller shall retain title to goods until payment of the full purchase price, subject to allocation of payments and release of security interest as required by law. The undersigned agrees to safely keep the goods, free from other liens and encumbrances at the below address, and not remove goods without consent of Seller.

Buyer agrees to execute all financing statements as may be required of Seller to perfect this conditional sales agreement.

At the election of Seller, the Buyer shall keep goods adequately insured, naming Seller loss-payee.

The full balance shall become due on default; with the undersigned paying all reasonable attorneys fees and costs of collection. Upon default, Seller shall have the right to retake the goods, hold and dispose of same and collect expenses, together with any deficiency due from Buyer; but subject to the Buyer's right to redeem pursuant to law and the Uniform Commercial Code.

THIS IS A CONDITIONAL SALE AGREEMENT.

Accepted:

_____   _____

Seller   Buyer

                               _____

                               Address

                               By_____

Record this Agreement or Financing Statement as required by state law to protect your rights.

CONSIGNMENT AGREEMENT

Consignment agreement made this   day of
               by and between   (Consignor),
and   (Undersigned).

1. Undersigned acknowledges receipt of goods as described on annexed schedule. Said goods shall remain property of Consignor until sold.

2. The Undersigned at its own cost and expense agrees to keep and display the goods only in its place of business, and agrees, on demand made before any sale, to return the same in good order and condition.

3. The Undersigned agrees to use its best efforts to sell the goods for the Consignor's account on cash terms, and at such prices as shall from time to time be designated by Consignor.

4. The Undersigned agrees, upon sale, to maintain proceeds due Consignor in trust, and separate and apart from its own funds and deliver such proceeds, less commission, to Consignor together with an accounting within   days of said sale.

5. The Undersigned agrees to accept as full payment a commission equal to   % of the gross sales price exclusive of any sales tax, which the Undersigned shall collect and remit.

6. The Undersigned agrees to permit the Consignor to enter the premises at reasonable times to examine and inspect the goods, and reconcile an accounting of sums due.

7. The Undersigned agrees to issue such financing statements for public filing as may reasonably be required by Consignor.

8. This agreement shall be binding upon and inure to the benefit of the parties, their successors and assigns.

_____   _____

Record in public filing office

Index

||||➡ ⬅||||